"Kat Armas does in *Sacred Belonging* exactly what she does best: leading us to tender and compelling questions while taking us on an inspired journey with the Sacred. Weaving stories of everyday life with thoughtful examinations of Scripture, Armas reminds us that our very lives are connected to the way we understand the Sacred around us and within us, which affects the way we treat one another and Mother Earth. Armas is a theological leader in fierce truth-telling and compelling story-sharing, and we should join her on this journey to reimagine what belonging could be."

—**Kaitlin Curtice**, award-winning author of *Native* and *Living Resistance*

"What a delicious book *Sacred Belonging* is. Yes, it's a devotional, but it's so much more than that. We are invited to taste and see biblical narratives with a new palate that decenters and decolonizes and disrupts limited ways of knowing. I read thankful for Kat's daughter, for the stretch marks she gave her mom, and the baby breath on her mom's neck, and the cooing that was music to Kat's ear as she sat before Holy to write. I read thankful for her partner, Taylor; for her mother; for her posse; for Kat's position in the world. Thankful for her eyes and heart in this moment, which though fraught and frightening, is where we sit, where we belong, yearning for better. I read thankful for the circumstances that put such beauty in Kat's holy imagination. I read thankful for this foretaste of glory divine. And you will too."

—**Rev. Dr. Jacqui J. Lewis**, senior minister, Middle Church; author of *Fierce Love*

"Kat Armas is the theologian we need, and *Sacred Belonging* is the devotional we've been waiting for. Rooted in and informed by Scripture, she shows us intuitive ways of communing with God through common things like water, pets, dreams, birthing, and the passage of time. I am stunned silent by this beautiful, relevant work."

—**Emily P. Freeman**, *Wall Street Journal* bestselling author of *The Next Right Thing*

T0051336

"Through beautiful stories interwoven with Scripture, Kat Armas has given us a devotional worth reading. She offers new perspectives rather than settling for conventional ones, casting a gentle but prophetic vision for a hopeful and decolonized faith. Kat invites us to see God differently. As for me: invitation accepted."

—**Peter Enns**, author of *Curveball*; host of *The Bible for Normal People* podcast

"*Sacred Belonging* is a devotional for all of us who feel cringey about devotionals. I couldn't stop highlighting and felt so held and respected by these words. The genius of this book is its author's generosity. Kat Armas gently and fiercely invites us into the story where Divine Love still speaks through the Scriptures to our souls, shaping us into people who know we are so loved that we can risk remembering that everyone and everything belongs."

—**K.J. Ramsey**, trauma therapist; author of *The Book of Common Courage* and *The Lord Is My Courage*

"Armas offers an imperative spiritual balm to some of us who have experienced Scripture in ways that have been demeaning, dehumanizing, isolating, and used solely to reprimand and not to restore. In *Sacred Belonging*, the space to explore and wonder brought a calming peace over my anxious mind. *Sacred Belonging* is an invitation into a deep, expansive, and healing way of encountering Scripture in a truly meaningful and transformative manner. Armas has a gentle way of guiding you and inviting you to 'go deeper,' just as Jesus has always invited us to do."

—**Arielle Estoria**, poet, author, and actor

SACRED
BELONGING

Also by the Author

Abuelita Faith: What Women on the Margins Teach Us about Wisdom, Persistence, and Strength

SACRED BELONGING

A 40-DAY DEVOTIONAL ON THE LIBERATING HEART OF SCRIPTURE

KAT ARMAS

BrazosPress

a division of Baker Publishing Group
Grand Rapids, Michigan

Published by Brazos Press
a division of Baker Publishing Group
Grand Rapids, Michigan
www.brazospress.com

Printed in the United States of America

Library of Congress Cataloging-in-Publication Data
Names: Armas, Kat, 1989– author.
Title: Sacred belonging : a 40-day devotional on the liberating heart of scripture / Kat Armas.
Description: Grand Rapids, Michigan : Brazos Press, a division of Baker Publishing Group, [2023] | Includes bibliographical references.
Identifiers: LCCN 2023002050 | ISBN 9781587435096 (paperback) | ISBN 9781587435997 (casebound) | ISBN 9781493440290 (ebook) | ISBN 9781493440306 (pdf)
Subjects: LCSH: Bible—Devotional literature.
Classification: LCC BS491.5 .A76 2023 | DDC 242/.5—dc23/eng/20230518
LC record available at https://lccn.loc.gov/2023002050

Published in association with Books & Such Literary Management, www.booksandsuch.com

Baker Publishing Group publications use paper produced from sustainable forestry practices and post-consumer waste whenever possible.

23   24   25   26   27   28   29   7   6   5   4   3   2   1

To Miss Lady Oak,
who towers above my home like a promise.
Thank you for your inspiration.
May your days continue to be long and fruitful,
even after we're gone.

CONTENTS

THE BODY

WISDOM

THE FEMININE

ACKNOWLEDGMENTS

Taylor, the words I write on this page cannot even begin to describe the work you put in to make this book come to life. Lord knows it wasn't easy for either of us. There have been so many sacrifices. So many sleepless nights. Thank you for figuring this thing out with me—how to be parents while pursuing passions and goals and dreams. Thank you for late nights editing these pages after you finished your own work. Thank you for late nights staying up to soothe our baby so I could wake up early to write. Thank you for your commitment to me and your support of my work. Thank you for being my sounding board, my safe space where these ideas could simmer and flourish. I know this thing has my name on it, but it is just as much yours as it is mine.

Mom, for every plane you boarded, every Uber you rode in, every diaper you changed, every meal you cooked, every snuggle you gave, every inch of floor you swept and mopped, every dish you washed—for every time you played with dogs and fed the cat—I owe you a world of gratitude. This book would be nothing without your selfless service to my family. Thank you for giving of yourself so this book could come to life.

Ash, your presence in my life through the hard things—like writing a book—sustains me. Thank you for seeing me through it.

Yetz, Nicole, Esther, Naty, your support in all my endeavors, your checking in on me constantly, and your love have kept me going.

Kim, Kelly, Jayshree, thank you for crying with me when I thought I couldn't finish this book and celebrating with me when I did.

Not Ladies (you know who you are), thank you for inviting me to be a part of our group. I am a better creative thanks to you all.

And ultimately, thanks to my daughter. You have given me new eyes from which to see, a new language from which to speak. Every word of this is for you.

INTRODUCTION

I must admit, I haven't read a devotional in years.

They've often felt, for me, like just another thing I must commit to in order to sustain a relationship with a God who lives primarily "in my heart." Devotionals have often pointed me toward what I need to change about myself or what I need to do to be better. To be sure, there are always ways we can grow, things we would do well to change. But perhaps as an alternative to simply focusing on ourselves, we ought to look at the bigger picture—recognizing that we belong to a web of life that is sacred and divine and holy. We are part of something that is far greater than us alone. We are creatures both brilliant and ignorant, significant and insignificant: broken, whole, and healing.

It is Easter Sunday as I write this, the resurrection of Jesus fresh in my mind. And I'm thinking about the words held close on the hearts of the characters in the resurrection story, words that changed everything for them.

"Don't be afraid." (Matt. 28:5)

"Why are you crying?" (John 20:15)

"Who are you looking for?" (John 20:15)

"Put your finger here. Look at my hands." (John 20:27)

I sit in the weight of these words trying to formulate my own, moved by the reality that these words tell a story of a God who doesn't expect us to be anything more or anything less than what we are— whether we are fearful or sad, searching or doubtful.

In this way, the bodily resurrection of Jesus is an invitation to be fully human.

That's what this devotional is about: being human. And with our humanity comes the ability to inquire, to imagine, to dream, to create.

When it comes to Scripture, I wonder what kind of relationship many of us would have to the text if we had all been invited to do those things when we read it. Rather than viewing the Bible as a book of absolutes, what if we were to read it as a diverse book of stories and instructions relating to the human experience in all its messiness and beauty? One of my seminary professors once said that when we read the Bible, we should read it with resistance: constantly asking questions, wrestling with it the way Jacob wrestled with God. May these pages invite you to do just that.

Asian feminist scholar Kwok Pui-lan offers a "postcolonial imagination" as a way of approaching our Bible reading with a "desire, a determination, and a process of disengagement from the whole colonial syndrome."[1] I argue that such a syndrome has permeated our being, causing us to view the world as fixed, linear, dichotomous, and functioning in hierarchical relationships of domination and submission. For many of us, the assumptions behind how we perceive the biblical text have brought us to a place of unlearning and unraveling—of decolonizing—where we find ourselves hungry for new, liberating insights into our faith tradition.

With this, two key questions emerge: First, how can the Bible and its tradition speak into today's questions? And second, can we reimagine the biblical world so as to have new horizons opened to us?

The Bible has played a major role in modern colonial relations. It has been used to legitimize the oppression that came from imperial domination of Indigenous populations around the globe. Thus, the Bible became a text of Western imperialism. When the Bible's content, which deals with every aspect of life—political, economic, religious, and historical—was taken out of its original context, the result yielded a depoliticized Bible and, as a consequence, religion in the West was reduced to personal faith and salvation. This allowed Western imperial culture to see anyone outside of its bounds as "other," including the very group to which Jesus belonged: the Jews. The writings of subjected people resisting empire became the very texts used to justify it.[2]

To decolonize the Bible and the ways it has shaped us, we must be able to imagine alternative perspectives that make possible a change in these power dynamics. This process emphasizes interpretations that are found on the periphery rather than center stage—leading us beyond the familiar to in-between places, places where new ways of thinking and seeing color our reality. To decolonize, we must engage every aspect of life, queering boundaries, and allowing new possibilities to emerge. We must, as activist Carol Adams says, "not dematerialize the sacred or despiritualize matter."[3]

●·●·●

This book is divided into five sections: creation, spirit, the body, wisdom, and the feminine. With an emphasis on these five themes, I invite you on a forty-day journey of repatterning, reimagining, and reweaving Scripture. Some reflections exegete well-known passages in a new light, while others center on telling a story—mostly bits and pieces of my own. I reflect on how I have come to understand the ways that the intricacies of daily life and faith are intertwined. My hope is that my musings might stir up something relatable, whether you align with my thinking or not. This is how theology is done: en conjunto. It is the work of a collective people coming together in their differences and disagreements, seeking to make sense of themselves, the world, and the divine.

Some of my reflections offer questions to ponder. Others don't. Feel free to read this as you wish. You can reflect on each theme or move around as you please. There is no right or wrong way to engage.

You may notice that I acknowledge the existence of deities found in pre-Christian or Indigenous spiritual traditions. This notion was not uncommon in the ancient world, as plenty of Israelites didn't deny other gods existed; they simply believed their God was the only deity worthy of worship.[4] Understanding this can offer us a liberative shift in our mindset and in our thinking, encouraging us to see that we are always perceiving God from our own setting and cultural moment. With this in mind, we are more able to approach diverse cultural beliefs with a posture of respect and understanding, which can awaken in us the audacity to believe that divine wisdom can be found in places we haven't been trained to look. You might also notice that in certain places I refer to "Spirit" without including the accompanying article.

To me, this sounds more intimate, like Spirit is a personal name. It is also a way of communicating that there are many ways to understand and experience the Spirit of the divine.

I also point you to things Native peoples and those living in the ancient world would have found meaning in—things modern Christians generally dismiss or avoid, such as the stars, the cycles of the moon, the four cardinal directions, and so on. It is in reflecting on these that we may find God speaking through creation in fresh ways, in Scripture and beyond.

While I focus on my own experience as a woman, the feminine does not refer only or specifically to women. In colonial thinking, femininity—in contrast to masculinity—has been attached to weakness and inferiority. Decolonizing invites us to wrestle with the feminine within us and also within the divine in order to get a fuller glimpse of both.

My hope is that these words will point you to a belonging deeper than you have dreamed of, that you will see and experience yourself being tethered to your ancestors, to God, and to every created thing. And in exploring this relationality, I also hope that you will get to know divinity as embodied—where you can find a God who is familiar with planting and sewing, good wine and lilies. This is the God to whom we belong: one who is wholly material and wholly spiritual. As close to us as our own skin and far beyond anything our minds can fathom. It is in this paradox where we exist, where our spiritualities find their home. This is where we find sacred belonging.

CREATION

Day 1

Sacred Belonging

All go to the same place;
all come from dust,
and to dust all return.

—Ecclesiastes
3:20 (NIV)

We got the news late one Sunday morning in mid-July that my father-in-law had died unexpectedly.

The phone rang loudly that day. Not only did the noise startle my spouse, Taylor, and me as we prepared to head out to grab lunch, but it also disrupted our lives—steering us in an unexpected direction—the way those dreaded phone calls always do. As soon as Taylor answered, we knew it was bad news. His grandfather's words pulsed through the phone like a heartbeat: "It's your dad. He's gone. I'm so sorry." I felt my heart sink deep into my body, where our daughter had been growing for seven months. Taylor's pale skin began losing its pink hue, the room starkly silent, except for his shallow breathing. I threw my arms around his chest as if to catch him, but my pregnant belly got in the way. After he hung up the phone, we lingered for what seemed like hours before Taylor packed up the car and made the difficult drive to the small country house where his father had raised him.

My father-in-law lived alone, nestled in a few acres of rural land, unburdened by the glare of city lights or the numbing buzz of cars and construction. The first time I visited, the quiet was so loud it made my ears ring as if they were detoxing. It was uncomfortable, but I didn't resist. I knew I needed it.

It was this quiet—and the simplicity that comes with it, I imagine—that enamored my father-in-law to life in the countryside. That kind of life felt foreign to a city girl like me, but Taylor remembers it with fondness: spending weekends with his knees in the dirt and the soil underneath his fingernails—responding to the needs of the earth like a trusted friend. These are the virtues that formed him.

It came as no surprise, then, that his father was working outdoors when his time came: tending to his land with the same love and devotion he had for years. It wasn't until a few days later that his friends found him lying in the dirt. It was a kind of poetry, taking his final breath on the land he spent his life cultivating—a land that loved him back. It was this relationship that sustained him until his heart gave out. They say he was alone when he died, but I imagine he felt far from it in the presence of the oak tree that hovered above him like a protective guardian.

According to some Indigenous traditions, humans don't claim the land; it is the land that claims us. This is in stark contrast to a colonizing mindset that views land as a commodity to be staked out and sold off. I imagine my father-in-law knew this truth intimately, its power embracing him as he lay to rest as one with the earth that claimed him.

In the opening chapters of Genesis, the Bible affirms a mutual and cyclical relationship between dirt and our bodies. The Bible is far from a book of science, but both agree on this point. Science teaches us that all the elements that make up the human body are found in the soil. This is a testament to what we already know to be true: we belong to the earth, and she belongs to us too.

● ● ● ● ● ● ●

The "balance of nature" is one of the earliest—and most widely known—theories about the natural world proposed by philosophers and scientists. It suggests that all things are held in a delicate balance with every other entity, with each entity so finely and intricately interwoven that if one is added or taken away, things can potentially go awry. Take, for instance, the case of the decimation of wolves in Yellowstone National Park.

In the 1920s, wolves in Yellowstone were eradicated due to pressure from ranchers worried about their livestock.[1] Before long, elk numbers increased because their predators were gone. But more elk meant that grass and saplings were overgrazed. Soon beavers disappeared and the riverbanks were left barren. The entire landscape was decimated, killing off species of birds that relied on the foliage for nesting. Because there was no longer any plant life to protect the ground, flooding washed away the soil and erosion progressed, changing the flow of rivers.

This extraordinary course of events was all due to the eradication of wolves, their place in the ecosystem so crucial that eliminating them meant rivers changed course and certain species could no longer survive there.[2]

Everything has a place in the ecosystem; however, the balance of nature theory has also been challenged by ecologists who claim that human activity constantly disturbs the environment. These disturbances (like killing off wolves in Yellowstone) lead to chaotic and dynamic changes, yet they purport that this is the norm in nature. Because humans are an unpredictable part of the ecosystem, a new equilibrium occurs when habitats change—although not necessarily for the better. In recognition of this, humans reintroduced wolves in Yellowstone in 1995, stabilizing its ecosystem once again.

Our world is both stable *and* chaotic, balanced *and* dynamic. Both states exist together yet still affirm the truth that we are part of a web of diversity that needs every creature—from beetle to elephant to deciduous leaf—to function in its fullness. Caring about deforestation and the loss of animal species is a worthwhile endeavor because everything responds to everything else. What happens to the earth happens to us.

In Matthew's Gospel, the story goes that when Jesus was dying, the earth went dark for three hours (27:45). At the moment he cried out and took his last breath, the land shook and the rocks split (27:51). Some interpreters might say this speaks to the supremacy of Jesus over creation, and maybe that's true—particularly when read through a Western lens of hierarchy. But perhaps it's more than that. In Colossians, Paul says that in Jesus all things are held together (1:17), so would it be farfetched to think that the cosmos would tumble into a kind of chaos at his death? I like to imagine that the earth was responding to her relationship to Jesus in a divine connection of sorts.

Through Jesus, God became one with us in this intricate web of life, experiencing alongside us the fullness of what it means to be human.

Perhaps the death of Jesus is also a lesson about the interdependency of all things.

Indeed, nothing happens in our world that doesn't affect something else. When wolves were eliminated, rivers changed course and bird species died out. When Jesus took his final breath, the earth shook and the rocks split. Our world and everything in it tell a story of belonging—a belonging established at the very beginning, in accordance with God's desire for all of creation to be in concert together.

●··●··●

A few days after Taylor's dad died, we found ourselves drowning in paperwork, account numbers, phone calls, and grief. We woke up early one morning and took the long stretch of rural country road to the courthouse to continue figuring out all the things you need to figure out after a parent dies unexpectedly. During this silent drive, we saw a billboard that read, *God recycles. He made you from dust.*

We laughed. It felt so fitting.

From dirt we come and to dirt we will return.

It is through the dirt that we are bound together in a sacred belonging.

- Reflect on the last time you felt like you belonged to a web of life larger than yourself.
- What cultivates belonging in your life?
- What can you nurture with your own hands that connects you to our ecosystem?

Day 2

The Creatures Teach Us

🌿

Look at the birds in the sky.
—Matthew 6:26

The first thing Jesus does after he is baptized is go into the wilderness to fast. Mark says that while he's there, he's with the wild animals and the angels. I often wonder if this is where Jesus's connection with the wild took root. From mountains to trees to vineyards, Jesus was a person in tune with his surroundings and aware of the natural world. His teachings were deeply rooted in the land and the wisdom found in the earth and her creatures.

No created thing was void of value or purpose for Christ. Fish and seeds had the potential to teach the most important things about loving neighbors and taking care of the poor. Observe the birds, Jesus advised, notice the lilies of the field (Matt. 6:26, 28). What if we took him seriously in our daily routines and did just that? What if we truly considered what wisdom might be found in all created things?

● ● ● ● ● ●

It was early spring when we moved into our first home in Tennessee. The flowers had just begun to bud and the birds to nest. I was doing my own nesting too—unpacking my belongings from boxes while my belly grew rounder and fuller each day. Life was flourishing around me and within me.

Taylor and I often spent our mornings sitting in foldable camping chairs in our backyard, watching the sun peek over our wooden fence, the steam rising from our cups of coffee, the oak trees towering above our heads. It was quiet and pleasant. Until it wasn't.

Our peaceful mornings ended when we realized we weren't alone in our new house. A family of starlings had made the wooden slabs of our carport their home before we moved in, and they made sure we knew it. Each day as we sat to enjoy the morning, we were met with the fury of parent starlings perched above our heads tirelessly squawking at the top of their little bird-lungs in an attempt to defend their space. I thought their behavior was poetic at first—a lesson in parenting as I prepared to become a parent myself. A reminder of God as a mother bird, perhaps, protecting her young. But these sentiments quickly changed when I could no longer relax in my own backyard.

"What kind of birds are those?" I asked Taylor one morning, frustrated.

"Oh, those are starlings."

"What do you know about them?"

"Well, I know they're annoying."

We laughed. A quick Google search informed me that "how to stop starlings from nesting on my roof" is a common concern among folks on the internet. Not only are they ubiquitous and invasive, but starlings are also known for being loud and obnoxious wherever they find themselves.

In addition to validating my irritation, I learned that starlings are able to mimic most sounds they hear: from car alarms to human speech, regularly embedding sounds from their surroundings into their own calls. In fact, their diverse and complex vocalizations make starlings a popular subject of research into the evolution of human language.

The sound of the starling is so unique one even became a muse to Mozart. He was so enthralled by a starling he heard at a pet store, Mozart brought it home and fashioned some of his music after its songs.[1] Learning this amused me. Perhaps it's no coincidence that some of the most hated birds in our midst have also served as inspiration for the world's most renowned musical compositions.

Suddenly I find myself marveling at the starling, remembering Jesus's invitation to notice the birds of the air (Matt. 6:26). So I started doing just that. I watched the starling for weeks, whispering *good morning* to her each day. She watched me back—a simple kind of reciprocity. I soon began to appreciate her forwardness, her insistence that I notice her.

This is what I love most about Jesus: he had a knack for always pointing us to the overlooked—from the human sitting in the corner to the creature squawking from her nest. They're there, they've always been there, but Jesus invites us to notice, to look closely.

One of my favorite examples of this is found in the story of the poor widow who put everything she had into the collection box of the temple treasury. The narrative begins by saying that Jesus sat and observed how the crowd was giving their money (Mark 12:41–44). I wonder what specific things Jesus was looking for. Was it her? Or was he simply observing, as he often did, noticing the things we tend to miss: the birds, the poor, the flowers? After seeing what she has done, Jesus calls the disciples over and encourages them to observe her too.

I've heard countless sermons praising this woman for her sacrificial giving and prompting that we should do the same. But when I read this story, I don't discern Jesus telling the disciples, "Do what she does." Instead, I discern Jesus saying first and foremost, "Look at this woman." Jesus wasn't giving the disciples a guilt trip, as might be implied. Instead, he invited them simply to notice—the disregarded, the pushed aside, the last people we'd look to for wisdom. *Pay attention to her.*

Barbara Brown Taylor notes that in order to see all there is to see, we must learn to look at the world not just once but twice.[2] The kin-dom of God is this way: hidden in plain sight (see invitation 7 for more on the kin-dom of God). And Jesus beckons us to look and then look closer.

But this kind of awareness doesn't come easy. To learn from what nature is telling us, we have to stop long enough to notice—to observe, to listen to how it might be speaking or what it might be teaching us—and this cannot be done with an oversaturated mind. Richard Rohr comments that noticing the natural world "takes contemplative practice, stopping our busy and superficial minds long enough to see the beauty, allow the truth, and protect the inherent goodness of what it is—whether it profits me, pleases me, or not."[3]

I think Job was privy to this. He may be known for his unrelenting faith in God, but Job stands out to me because of the way he understood the natural world. When his friend tells him to repent so that his fortune will be restored, Job reminds him that divine wisdom can be found in the places we aren't trained to look. Job says, "Ask Behemoth and he will teach you, the birds in the sky, and they will tell you; or talk to earth, and it will teach you; the fish of the sea will recount it for you" (Job 12:7–8).

Scripture reminds us that divine wisdom flows through all created things if we're willing to listen. We can discover much from plants and animals that know the intimate details of survival and flourishing. This is one of the greatest parts of being human: finding kinship with all of creation as we learn more about ourselves and the divine.

It's important to understand how the natural world communicates to us. Oftentimes, we tend to reduce both people and nature to empty vessels—listening only for what God might speak *through* them instead of what wisdom they might be imparting themselves. As Anishinaabe writer Patty Krawec observes, "Listening only for what God might be saying through something diminishes our investment in the world around us and disconnects us from everything, including people, because we don't listen to them either."[4]

●··●··●

After advising his followers to notice the birds of the air, Jesus continues his teaching: "They don't sow seed or harvest grain or gather crops into barns. Yet your heavenly Father feeds them. Aren't you worth much more than they are?" (Matt. 6:26). Through the eyes of Jesus, we get a glimpse of the value of the natural world and the beauty he sees in it.

Sure, a human life is valued more than a bird's life, according to Jesus, but this doesn't mean that birds have no worth. In fact, his point rests on the truth that birds, too, have value. That each one is taken care of by God and provided for.

If anything, it's the birds that remind us that we are worthy.

My neighbor the starling did just that— demanding I notice her and her young. She squawked her truth, reminding me of her value and of my own.

- What wisdom has the natural world communicated to you, whether about herself, yourself, or about the divine?
- How might you engage in the kind of awareness that Jesus had? Where might you take the opportunity to notice, to observe, and to listen?

The Mountains Groan

We know that the whole creation is groaning together and suffering labor pains up until now.

—Romans 8:22

I am standing almost fifteen thousand feet above sea level, nearly a week into a hike I was not prepared to undertake. My feet are blistered, and my body is in so much pain from climbing that I am numb. We were about twelve hours from the summit, and I had lagged behind the group. My Miami-attuned lungs, not used to the high elevation, weren't cooperating. With every failed deep breath I attempted to take, my lungs wheezed as if to plead with me, *we belong in the tropics*. This terrain was not the terrain of my ancestors. But my tour guide and new friend Manco—a native to this land—showed me the way, offering patience and generosity every time my pace slowed down. When I stopped to gather my breath, he'd stop too, pulling coca leaves out of his pocket and rubbing them in his palms like a potion, gesturing for me to inhale. "Breathe," he'd say, drawing the word out as he exhaled.

Raw coca leaves were sacred to the Incas because of their healing properties, and they are still an integral part of Peruvian national heritage—particularly when treating altitude sickness. My eyes lit up every time I inhaled from his worn hands and felt the oxygen fill the deep crevices of my lungs. Manco would laugh, satisfied. "The earth heals us," he'd remind me. It seemed to please him to share with me the wisdom of that place. The earth—his earth—was saving me, and I think that made him proud.

● ● ◦ ● ◦ ●

About fifty miles northwest of Cuzco, Peru, high up in the Andes, sits Machu Picchu, the ancient Incan citadel built in the fifteenth century. This "wonder of the world" is believed to have been the home of Emperor Pachacuti and draws over a million tourists every year to its breathtaking landscape.

Before visiting in 2015, I researched the multiple ways to get to the site, one of which is the Salkantay Trail, which takes you to the base of the city. I didn't have much hiking experience but decided to take this route to get the best vantage of the Andes in all their glory. I should've been a bit more prepared.

The journey took several days of trekking through rugged terrain, from cloud forests to lush jungles. During the day, we walked for dozens of miles at steadily increasing elevation, passing waterfalls and grazing sheep. At night we slurped stew from a community pot and slept on the dirt, under the stars.

Accompanied by those native to the mountains, we learned that Salkantay means "wild mountain" in Quechua, the Incas' native language. The Incas believed that each mountain has its own spirit. According to their mythology, apus (mountain spirits) protect nearby territories and inhabitants, including cattle and crops. The most significant apus are associated with the highest Peruvian mountains, Salkantay being the second most important. Learning this helped me recognize the great honor it was to be in her midst. If you've ever stood among the mountains, you may have experienced a sense of this—the rush of an energy beyond your own that shallows your breath and makes your heart skip a few beats.

One morning, as we neared the summit, I began to hear a strange rumbling in the air that did not belong, something that seemed improbable. *Jets?* I wondered to myself, confused. *What are jets doing out here?* When I turned to look for the source of the intensifying roar, instead of a plane I saw birds. I realized what I was hearing was not a jet but the sound of wings ripping through the air—a sound I did not know existed. It was otherworldly, almost too overwhelming to bear. I sat down on the nearest rock and cried. Manco looked over at me.

"The mountain is speaking to you?" he asked.

I nodded.

"Good. It means you're listening."

The energy changed when we finally arrived at Machu Picchu. More breathtaking than the views is the ancient architecture. The massive blocks manipulated into walls and temples and towers (without the use of mortar) have left archaeologists speechless. Their feats of engineering have earned the Incas classification as one of the most advanced early civilizations in the world.

Our marveling at the site was tempered by the heaviness in the voices of some of our guides as they taught us about how Machu Picchu was abandoned by the Incas shortly before European conquistadors arrived, which is probably why it was left undiscovered and relatively untouched for so long. This didn't stop the effects of the Spanish conquest, however, as the Inca population was eradicated by smallpox due to interactions with the colonizers.

"The mountains tell their own stories. Sometimes their stories are of beauty and sometimes of pain," they told us.

The beauty of Machu Picchu doesn't erase the stench of death that marks the scenery. Perhaps it even intensifies it. Standing in the presence of the mountains, I wondered how the apus felt about the mistreatment the original inhabitants and caretakers endured. Did they grieve the injustices the earth herself experienced?

The space once sacred was now becoming a resource for consumption. Before the COVID-19 pandemic slowed tourism down, the ruins and the infrastructure were being overwhelmed. Machu Picchu continues to suffer harm from an economy of extraction.

I lagged behind the group again (this time on purpose) and sat by yet another rock to cry. This time with feelings of heaviness over death, decay, and exploitation. I grieved the system that had led me there in the first place.

My friend Manco joined me on the stone.

"You know what this means?" he whispered.

I'm listening.

●··●··●

Paul describes creation as groaning alongside humanity in his letter to the Romans—those living in the epicenter of empire and antagonized daily by the woes of imperialism. At the heart of every empire is an insatiable desire to rule over the natural world and every creature living within it. The Roman Empire, specifically, not only wanted to restructure and remake the whole world, but its rulers believed they had already ushered forth the golden age of peace and prosperity.[1]

Paul's powerful image tells of the shared grief we experience in concert with the planet, but what makes his words subversive is the fact that he uses imperialistic language to construct a worldview that opposes imperial ideology. In doing this, Paul envisions a new world—one remade not by the empire but by God.

Much like empires today, the Roman Empire set out to ravage the world through military domination and economic exploitation. It destroyed entire cities, deforested mountains, depleted fields once ripe for harvest, and polluted water once teeming with food and drink. In response, the cosmos cried out in pain. Paul's personification of the earth tells the story of "a holistic, interdependent system with a life and development of its own."[2]

For Paul, the earth is our kin, groaning alongside of us. This declaration subverts imperial logic that didn't—and still doesn't—care about or value creation. According to the book of Romans, both humans and the natural world share in the longing for new life. This is true across history, as the suffering of people and the suffering of land have always gone together. Indeed, advocating for justice for the land and advocating for justice for humankind are not separate endeavors. When the land suffers, so do those who depend on it. When we protest and fight against the devastation of the earth, we are doing so for the dignity of the people who live on it.

The Bible affirms this. Leviticus 25:2 commands that the land itself must observe a Sabbath. The idea is that the land is to be maintained so that it remains just as fertile when passed on as it was when received.[3] The intent was that the land would continue to produce for the long haul—for future generations—and support sustainable farming practices, which inevitably helps the poor.

Throughout the Bible, the natural world joins both God and the prophets in bearing witness against humanity's evils and injustices. Isaiah, Micah, Hosea, and Jeremiah all describe the earth's mourning and languishing caused by the burden of human exploitation. Our world has so much to grieve: the injustice toward her inhabitants, the eradication of her kin. We kill not only each other but also the very place we call home.

But we are not alone in our lament. God mourns with us: "I will weep and wail for the mountains," God says in Jeremiah 9:10, "and lament for the grazing lands in the wilderness. They are dried up and deserted; no sound of the flocks is heard; no sign of birds or animals is seen; all have vanished."

What is our truest response but, like God, to grieve?

Eco-philosopher Joanna Macy explains that grief is a doorway into a deeper understanding of life, identity, and interconnectedness. "The most important thing we can do for the sake of our planet is to hear within ourselves the sounds of the earth crying." She goes on to echo the words of Buddhist monk Thich Nhat Hanh, "Until we can grieve for our planet we cannot love it—grieving is a sign of spiritual health."[4]

Grief can seem pitiful, offensive, or inconvenient to some Christians, as it has nothing to do with a victorious God. To those who have embraced an imperial Christ, grief is weakness. But this is precisely why we need to grieve: as resistance and as a spiritual practice. We need "tears that cleanse," as Macy says. Our grief "is not a private burden but a shared experience on this planet."[5]

So let us lament. *It means we're listening.*

Day 4

A Wild World beyond Us

Is it due to your understanding that the hawk flies,
spreading its wings to the south?
Or at your command does the eagle soar,
the vulture build a nest on high?

—Job 39:26–27

I opened my front door, exasperated at the yapping of my dog, Rogelio. The sun had set, and dusk was settling over our snow-covered lawn. I was dealing with those evening hours with a newborn when their seemingly insatiable hunger strikes for hours on end. I dreaded the evenings those first few weeks postpartum, and the furry little life in our home, dependent on us and loyal to us, didn't make things easier. I'm ashamed to admit he had begun to feel like a burden: demanding time and attention I could not give.

On this particularly cold night, Rogelio was relentless, and I could not coax him inside. I returned to my spot at the sink where I had been slurping reheated soup from a cardboard cup, a crying baby on my chest, while Taylor attempted to corral him back in the house. My meal was interrupted by a knock at the window, where Taylor beckoned me to join them. I peeked outside, finally catching a glimpse of what the commotion was about: a family of deer had wandered onto our front lawn.

When we joined Rogelio in the snow, he immediately stopped barking, satisfied we'd finally listened to him. The family of three seemed vigilant, but calm. They peered in our direction, curious. They didn't seem concerned, but I know I was. At the time, I lived only a few short blocks from downtown. Highways and main streets sprawled across my community like spiderwebs. Where did this family of deer come from? Did they walk down Shelby Avenue, romping through the street dodging cars? Were they in search of an adventure? Or simply lost?

We bundled up in blankets and watched them, wondering about their lives, making up stories about how they got here. They lingered for a while, and we lingered too. It was a sort of magic, being with these wild creatures that seemed so comfortable in our presence—strange behavior for prey animals that rely on their fear instinct for survival. The downtown lights twinkled in the distance; my soup got cold on the counter. I grabbed a handful of snow and tossed it across the yard. Rogelio ran to catch it. We held our baby close in the winter chill, and the demands of life melted away.

●··●··●

The last five chapters in the book of Job take us on a journey across the cosmos and past a myriad of sites and species—from the ocean to the heavens and into the wild. In Job 38–41, God asks Job a remarkable series of seventy-seven questions about the natural world. These questions remind Job and his friends that the workings of creation are beyond the boundaries of their limited knowledge.

"Have you gone to the sea's sources?" (38:16)

"Have you surveyed earth's expanses?" (38:18)

"Can you guide the stars at their proper times?" (38:32)

"Who put wisdom in remote places, or who gave understanding to a rooster?" (38:36)

"Did you give strength to the horse, clothe his neck with a mane?" (39:19)

What these questions make clear is how little is within our control and how our limitations restrict us from fully grasping the complexities of creation's domains. Our humanity diminishes our ability to truly appreciate the earth's expanses. As these chapters show, the natural world is full of mysteries that can never be dominated.

What response can be given other than to confess there are no answers for these questions? "I have indeed spoken about things I

didn't understand, wonders beyond my comprehension," Job says
(Job 42:3). Job's only choice is to recognize and affirm how vast,
beautiful, and incomprehensible our world is. To rest in this knowledge is a true gift. This is why assuming God was being brusque in
his questioning might do us a disservice. Perhaps God was offering
Job an opportunity to remember how wildly important and wildly
unimportant humans are at the exact same time. We humans are part
of a glorious world in which life is flourishing around us, indifferent
to our presence.

What a grace it is to remember that we are not the center of the
universe. I think this is part of what draws us to creation stories. In
the Genesis narrative, humans are the final characters to step into
the scene. The ocean and stars, the plants and animals are all created
first, existing and thriving before we even show up. This proclaims the
truth that while the natural world has lived—and can live—without
humans, humans cannot live without the natural world. We need her
for our most basic functions: to breathe and to eat. This fact alone
should inspire humility.

Both creation stories (as told in Gen. 1 and 2) are sacred declarations of our humble place on this planet. We enter the world and join
a web of relationships already formed, a conversation already taking
place—one beyond our understanding. Put on any nature documentary and most of us are instantly gripped by the way the wild world
communicates. Trees talk to one another via their roots, agreeing together on a "communal bloom strategy," synchronizing when they'll
produce fruit and when they'll rest.[1]

We know animals communicate too, but not just within their own
species. Interspecies friendships happen throughout the wild as relationships and bonds constantly form between unexpected friends. For
example, the hornbill birds of Africa warn mongooses of oncoming
danger from their predators, the raptors. As a result, mongooses delay
their foraging so hornbills can get in on the feast. Their relationship
is so intimate that mongooses feel comfortable letting their tiny pups
play at the feet of the hornbill—a would-be dinner for the bird.

This mutuality is found between wolves and ravens, too, among
countless other species. Wolves teach their pups to see ravens as
members of their community, working together for each other's good.

Ravens alert wolves of oncoming threats, and wolves thank them by allowing ravens to help themselves to their food.[2]

How do such vastly different species of animals learn these intricate systems of communication? The wisdom they hold is inexplicable.

Across time and history, native populations have known the wisdom of the natural world and respected their place within the ecosystem rather than seeing themselves as masters over it. But a shift occurred in our relationship to creation with the introduction of agriculture during the Stone Age (or the first agricultural revolution), when humans began domesticating animals and planting crops. Colonization and the "owning" of land, animals, and people only perpetuated the idea of domination as an inherent right. Before long, humans saw themselves as superior to all things in the natural world.

We would do well to consider that humans interact with only a fraction of the earth. "Consider the fact that there are places in the depth of the oceans, on the highest mountains, and deep in space that human beings have never seen and likely never will," writes Keetoowah Cherokee descendant Randy Woodley. There are places in our world unexplored by human hands, unseen by human eyes. "Such unreachable places seem to be reserved for the Creator's enjoyment and for other beings in creation—but not for humans."[3]

●··●··●

We thanked Rogelio for drawing our attention to the deer before we came inside, for reminding us that while what's happening within our walls is important, there is so much more happening in the world beyond. This brilliant planet survives and thrives, and much of it has absolutely nothing to do with us, other than to graciously teach us what it means to be human in relationship with the world.

Inside, the baby may have been crying or the dog incessantly barking, but outside? The insects were hibernating in tree trunks, and the mice were foraging for food. A family of deer might have been on an adventure and in as much awe of us as we were of them. The world moves and the world shifts and life happens beyond our door even if we don't take the time to notice.

But imagine if we did?

I still think about the deer on my front lawn often and, when I do, a sense of peace comes over me as I remember that we coexist in this wild world together. Looking into their eyes, we engaged in a conversation, a simple mutuality. A belonging that felt vaguely familiar.

I've since learned that as a matriarchal species, younger deer rely on the older females to cue them to danger. While deer are flinching at any sound or movement, the alpha doe remains calm, running *only* when she senses genuine danger. The mama deer must've sensed safety and peace in my home, in our home, in us. This was a gift I didn't know I needed at that moment, when life felt all but peaceful.

I wonder whether those deer found their way to a secluded spot. While I know I'll never see them again, the gift of their presence was a beckoning toward the divine, a gentle nudge to remember our humble place in this wonderful, wild world.

- How might remembering your humble place on this planet lead you to live a fuller life?
- How might this mutual interdependence encourage you to take better care of the planet and all the living things that depend on her for survival?

Day 5

Our Soulful Companions

The righteous care for the needs of their animals.

—Proverbs 12:10 (NIV)

When my cat Scully died unexpectedly on Mother's Day, I cried daily for six months. And what made it worse was that I felt embarrassed by this. A kindly "How are you?" sent me spiraling, as I'd find myself swatting tears from my face like mosquitos while muttering awkwardly, "I'm sorry, I know it's just a cat." But why should we feel foolish grieving the pets we've lost? As if our pets aren't part of our families; as if the intimacy we share—homes and beds and meals, difficult times and joyous ones, moves and life changes—don't warrant the pain we experience when the bond we've formed is suddenly untethered.

We know our animal kin are not *just* anything.

Sometimes they're everything.

Taylor bought me a massage to calm my nerves after we got the news that we wouldn't have Scully much longer. When I walked into the masseuse's office, she must've discerned that all was not well.

"How are you doing today?" she asked with a sincerity that broke me. I began to weep in front of this stranger. I apologized for my state over the news about my cat. But to my surprise, her eyes filled with tears too.

"I lost my pup recently. You don't need to apologize," she told me. And I cried even harder because there's nothing quite like being seen and understood.

As I walked out, she gave me the number of a vet who came to her home to put her dog down.

"When you're ready," she said.

I wasn't.

● ● ● ● ● ●

Will our pets be in heaven?

Every devoted pet owner has likely pondered this question, and if we had any proximity to the church growing up, we might have heard *no* and been told something about them not having souls.

Sure, animals might not experience life the same way we do—from what we can tell, they don't wonder about their place in the universe. But have you ever made amends with your dog after yelling at them for some sort of misbehavior? Search on YouTube for "dog feels guilty" and you'll probably be convinced our animals feel remorse—and understand when we say we're sorry too. This reciprocity with our animal kin secures our bond.

The prophet Isaiah describes the vision of a new earth where the wolf and the lamb lie down together (Isa. 11:6; 65:25). This is often interpreted as a sign that there will be no enmity between creatures—both human and nonhuman—in the afterlife, and this is true. But have you ever wondered what else this verse might imply? It seems wolves and lambs will be with us in eternity. So why not our soulful companions?

In chapter 60, Isaiah describes this new, future city, but this time there are more than animals. There are walls and gates and lumber and precious metals, and there are boats—the same boats that were in Tarshish. It makes me wonder why, then, we think only things with "souls" will have a place in this new age.

Besides, why do we assume animals don't have them?

The Hebrew word for soul is *nephesh*, and it's used 753 times in the Hebrew Scriptures. Genesis 2:7 says that God breathed life into the human, and the human became "a living soul" (*nephesh hayyah*). When God makes animals, it says they also have *nephesh hayyah* (Gen. 1:30). The same is true of all the sea animals and flying creatures as well as cattle, creeping things, and beasts.[1] According to Scripture, not only do our pets have souls, but so do eight-legged creatures and the fish that scour the bottom of the ocean.

The Bible is full of mystery.

There's an odd story in Numbers 22 about a talking donkey. His owner, Balaam, is known as an evil prophet. He's on his way to entice

Israel to sin when God sends an angel to intercept him. Balaam can't see the angel standing in the middle of the road, blocking the donkey's way. But the donkey can see it. Balaam beats his donkey three times for going off course and switching direction to go around the angel before "the LORD opened the donkey's mouth" (v. 28). She defends herself. She asks her owner what she has done to deserve being beaten. God then opens Balaam's eyes to see the angel in the road. The angel, too, asks, "Why have you beaten your donkey?" (v. 32).

At the surface, I love that this is what the angel is concerned about: fair treatment for this donkey. But more than that, the lesson is that the owner should have trusted his donkey. She asks him, "Am I not your donkey, on whom you've often ridden to this day?" (v. 30). There's a relationship there built on trust and mutuality. The animals we are bonded to in reciprocity are full of sacred and divine wisdom.

The desire for fair treatment of Balaam's donkey mirrors many of the instructions Israel was given about how they were to treat their own livestock. For example, animals were to be allowed rest on the Sabbath (Deut. 5:14), and the Israelites were not to muzzle their ox while it was treading out grain so that it could eat (25:4).

And in Genesis, after the flood, God makes a covenant not only with Noah but also with everything living (Gen. 9:13). This is curious as covenants are partnerships, two-way agreements that require consent from both parties. Perhaps there is something God is trying to communicate to us about the value of animals.

●··●··●

The following week, when Scully could barely move and her breathing began slowing down, we called the vet and scheduled for them to come and put her down peacefully, in our home. That night, we weren't sure if she'd make it until morning. I couldn't handle the thought that I might wake up to her lifeless body, so I asked Taylor to switch sides of the bed with me so that he could sleep next to her.

My girl noticed that I wasn't near her after only a few minutes. With the last ounce of energy she could muster in her dying body, she stood up and slowly climbed over Taylor, letting out heavy gasps from the effort it took her. She found her place next to me, spending her last night on earth curled up against her human.

I realized in that moment how afraid of death I was—so much so that I was willing to separate myself from her when I knew how badly she needed me. I spent the rest of that night reflecting on that fear, committing myself from that moment forward to a journey of growth and healing. And for that, I am forever indebted to Scully.

Oftentimes, our pets serve as our greatest teachers.

Richard Rohr dedicates his book *The Universal Christ* to his dog, writing, "Without an apology, lightweight theology, or fear of heresy, I can appropriately say that Venus was also Christ for me."[2] I know Rohr is not alone in this. If Jesus is found in the least of these, then it must mean he can be found in our animal kin too. Their presence in our lives teaches us something about love and about grace and about grief and about all the things it means to be human.

I wonder what our world would look like if we lived as if animals had souls? Perhaps then they wouldn't be shoved into factories, pumped with hormones, and resigned to tiny cages. What if we understood how we treat animals and how we treat each other are related—as people are also often forced to work in inhumane conditions? What kind of collective healing might we experience if we truly believed that *every* creature from the ant to the stray dog to our human neighbor carried a sacredness within them?

What might we experience of the depths and wonders and joys of God if we lived as though our animal kin spoke the language of Spirit too? What if when I looked into Scully's eyes as she took her last breath there was something in my soul that spoke to hers—something we shared as creatures of this earth?

Day 6

Creation Rejoices

Let all the rivers clap their hands;
   let the mountains rejoice out loud altogether before
   the LORD
   because he is coming to establish justice on the earth!
                                                —Psalm 98:8–9

Cloudy skies often feel like omens. Weather forecasts regularly lead to canceled plans, leaving us to watch the hours pass while we sit warm and dry in our homes. I wonder how many experiences I've missed while sheltered from the water that falls free from the sky.

There was one particularly hot and thick September day when a good friend and I stubbornly decided to go for a hike, even though pillows of gray hovered above us. We hoped we'd make it before the rain began to fall. The short and light, on and off sprinkles felt like a nice respite from the heat, so we committed to the trail, stopping every few minutes under an oak tree to swat mosquitos and take shelter from the drizzle.

It didn't take long, though, for the light drizzle to become a torrential downpour. Oak trees were no longer a refuge as their leaves bounced and danced in the torrent, pearls of water smacking us and the earth. We felt unsure at first as our feet sloshed in wet shoes, our hair stringy and soppy, sticking to our cheeks. We decided to make a run for shelter while clinging to one another like tree frogs. Catching each other's eyes midway through our sprint, we stopped in our tracks. Who were we kidding? We bent over in laughter, surrendering to the rain. The pitter-patter of the water was so loud that it drowned out our howls. We ambled along the rest of the way and experienced some of life's small pleasures: catching raindrops with our tongue, splashing in puddles like children, and twirling like dancers on a stage.

28

"There is no substitute for standing in the rain to waken every sense," says scientist and member of the Citizen Potawatomi Nation Robin Wall Kimmerer, "senses that are muted within four walls, where my attention would be on me instead of all that is more than me."[1]

That Sunday, we stopped being spectators of the rain and became a part of her symphony of celebration. Our joyful shrieks joined the hiss, hums, and dribbles of creation as water drops found their new home in the river and the soil. The rain was laughing with us too, and for a moment everything in us sprang to life.

●··●··●

Have you heard of the trees that giggle when they're caressed? It's true. The Gudgudi tree in Dudwha on the border of Nepal shakes its leaves when its trunk is stroked. I haven't stopped thinking about this since I learned of it.

We've been told that plants don't feel, but we know plants react to stimuli all the time. Consider the Venus flytrap, which snaps its leaves shut at the sense that lunch has arrived. Or the *mimosa pudica* plant I once encountered, which curled up when I touched her, hugged my finger when I said hello.

Plants surely feel things. We know the mountains grieve (recall the reflection for day 3); the flora wail along with us as glaciers melt and rainforests disappear. But that's not the entire story. If sorrow and joy are sisters—traveling together on this journey of life, accompanying one another through the terrible and the beautiful—then we know one cannot exist without the other. If creation groans, then mustn't it rejoice with us too? As my native Peruvian friend Manco reminded me, "Mountains tell their own stories—stories of both beauty and pain."

In Genesis, God asks Eve and Adam to look after creation: to enjoy the natural world, to know her, to trust her wisdom—and most importantly, to enter into relationship with her. But instead, Christianity perpetuated the logic of domination by misunderstanding the command in Genesis 1:26 that calls us to have "dominion over" life on earth. The word *dominion* in this context has long been misused by those hungry for power, looking for any excuse to exert control as they wish. It is often invoked to support the notions of conquering and enslavement—of plants, animals, and people. But what if our contemporary renderings of it have been misguided? Part of what makes *dominion* tricky to understand is the preposition translated in English as "over." A better one, suggests theologian Ellen Davis, is "among" or "with respect to." And while *dominion* has long been understood as *domination*, a more accurate definition is something akin to exercising "skilled mastery." This suggests "something like a craft or an art," says Davis, that considers the place of unique responsibility humans have in the cosmos.[2]

What many have failed to see is that humans aren't the only ones told to fill the earth. To "be fruitful and multiply" is a blessing given to animals and plants alike (Gen. 1:22). This is important because this blessing is what sets the condition for human exercise of skilled mastery. Human dominion cannot undo the prior blessing that all of creation is to flourish. If the natural world was to be fruitful and multiply, then our "dominion" over it should not hinder that command.

This is the honorable task we are given as a species—the responsibility to represent God's tender and compassionate "skilled mastery" with respect to the world. We are to stand for God's justice even when it stands in the way of our own self-interest.[3] Doing so leads not just to the flourishing of creation but to her rejoicing as well.

> Let the sea and everything in it roar;
>> the world and all its inhabitants too.
> Let all the rivers clap their hands;
>> let the mountains rejoice out loud altogether before the
>> LORD
>> because he is coming to establish justice on the earth!
>> (Ps. 98:7–9)

The psalmist proclaims the truth that if the world groans at injustice, then she rejoices at justice too. She claps her hands and opens her throat in a roar of satisfaction when we act in favor of her flourishing— from the plants and animals within her to the people who need her nourishment to survive. Caring for the earth is a moral concern for all of us. Theologian James Cone asserts that "a clean and safe environment is a human and civil rights issue." It is the poorest and most marginalized around us that suffer disproportionately from the harm done to our planet. He goes on, "If we do not save the earth from destructive human behavior, no one will survive. That fact alone ought to be enough to inspire people of all colors to join in the fight for a just and sustainable planet."[4]

●··●··●

My husband is cultivating a garden in our front lawn with trees and plants indigenous to the land. Our hope is that it will attract the animal life that is supposed to be here, the species who have called this place home long before we have. We do this so that the land and its kin may flourish long after we are gone. Every time we notice a new friend—be it a bee or a bird—we celebrate. It has found its way home.

We weep over an injured planet, but weeping for our lost landscapes is not enough. We must also sit in gratitude that this planet we've exploited still explodes with splendor, still sings with life. Embracing her beauty magnifies our own.

We put our hands in the dirt to make ourselves whole again. We plant native trees and beckon the bees to make a home with us. We welcome the insects and all who thrive from the wisdom of the land. We recycle and pick up trash with gratitude because, as Kimmerer writes, "Even a wounded world holds us, giving us moments of wonder and joy."[5] Our wounded world is still evidence of the divine, a blueprint and canvas of the holy.

We rejoice because God said it was good—all of it.

In Mark, Jesus tells his disciples to proclaim the good news to all creation, to every creature (16:15). I think how we nurture our world is part of what Jesus meant by this. Good news that has nothing to do with the flourishing of creation is no good news at all.

So let us sing with the trees and the birds. Let us dance in the rain. Let us proclaim our goodness together.

Day 7

A Kin-dom of Reciprocity

Jesus asked, "What is God's kingdom like? To what can I compare it? It's like a mustard seed that someone took and planted in a garden. It grew and developed into a tree and the birds in the sky nested in its branches."

—Luke 13:18–19

Outside my back door lives a complex food web—an active ecosystem contained within a plastic bin. From what can be visibly seen, this bin is filled with dirt, scraps of cardboard, fallen leaves, and food waste, but on a scale smaller than the naked eye can see, bacteria, fungi, and microbes are feeding and growing and thriving in their very own tiny community.

Every day or so after preparing our meals, we open the lid and drop in the scraps we've collected: fruit stems and peels, vegetable skins, coffee grounds, and eggshells, among other things. During one particularly rainy week, I opened the bin and found more than dirt and decomposing food. As can be expected, a grumble of maggots turned the purple, green, and red canvas into a slimy sea of white. It doesn't matter how many times I might run into them while on our composting journey, seeing these critters crammed into the two-foot enclosure always sends a chill down my spine. I slammed the lid shut so hard it knocked several of them from the lid down to join their friends in the dirt.

For the next few days, Taylor rolled his eyes and chuckled at me every time I set our scraps on the counter by the door and asked him to drop them in the bin. My Google search history was soon filled with "How do you get rid of maggots in your compost?" I acted as if they weren't supposed to be there, as if they didn't have a role, a purpose, or a job to do in the web of life—despite how gross and seemingly insignificant they were.

● ● ● ● ● ● ●

The disciples asked Jesus why he spoke in parables (Matt. 13:10). A good question: one we've probably all wondered about at some point. After learning a little bit more about parables, I'm convinced the answer lies in the high regard Jesus had for the people he encountered.[1] Jesus wasn't interested in singular, simplistic, black-and-white interpretations or clear-cut answers. He respected his hearers too much to make all his teachings that easily digestible. Instead, it seems Jesus spoke in parables because he wanted folks to wrestle with their spirituality. He expected those present not to simply listen to his teaching but to think and find their own understandings as well.

The meanings of Jesus's parables have been explained to us so many times, we've lost sight of their unusual nature. But for Jesus, God's kingdom never looked like what others expected it to. The disciples can attest to this, as they constantly misunderstood the lessons he sought to teach through them. Perhaps this is because the parables were intended not to make us comfortable, but to surprise, challenge, provoke, confront, disturb, and indict.[2]

This is the power and beauty of the kingdom of God: *it defies all expectations.*

Jesus compared the kingdom of God to a lot of strange and unconventional things. A mustard seed is one of the more surprising ones because it starts out as something small and seemingly ordinary and becomes something large and extraordinary. And while there is truth to this, the peculiar nature of parables makes me wonder whether this is really the primary point Jesus was trying to make.

The text says that the tiny mustard seed grew and developed into a tree. "And the birds in the sky nested in its branches" (Luke 13:19).

For the original listeners, this would have sounded bizarre. While mustard plants (which were common in the area) may have been seen as beneficial and not necessarily a nuisance, they still grew wild and untamable, making them difficult to get rid of. But stranger than the thought of planting one is the notion of a mustard seed growing into a large tree. You see, mustard seeds tend to grow more into shrubs or bushes than trees, and while birds *can* perch in them, they don't typically nest there.

So what is Jesus trying to communicate? Perhaps that small seeds, when left to germinate, have the potential to grow into great things that become a blessing to those we don't expect to be blessed. In the parable, mustard seeds become a blessing for birds the same way God's people are to be a blessing to others, and this happens out in the everyday world: in gardens, in nature, through trees, in what's already present around us. The kin-dom of God surprises, but often in very ordinary ways.

Jesus then tells another parable: the kingdom of God is like a little bit of yeast, which a woman took and hid in wheat until it worked its way through all the dough (Matt. 13:33; Luke 13:20–21). This short parable packs a heavy punch, as it probably would've been more shocking to original listeners than its prequel. When folks heard the phrase "the kingdom of God is . . ." they expected to hear about strong men and armies and power, so to hear that the kingdom of God is something like yeast that a woman uses to bake would have sent their minds spiraling, perhaps even offended. Most believed Jesus would deliver them from their enemies through a show of force. "Lord, are you going to restore the kingdom to Israel now?" the disciples asked Jesus after his resurrection (Acts 1:6). They wanted to know if it was finally time for him to enter the temple in power and glory, which is understandable for a people under the thumb of the Roman Empire. You can imagine their surprise and perhaps even their disgust when the kingdom of God is described not as powerful but as weak, vulnerable, and ordinary: *the kingdom of God is like a tiny bit of yeast a woman puts in dough and makes enough bread to feed her entire community.*

I imagine their sentiments are not unlike those of many people even today who also expect the kingdom of God to be mighty, militaristic, and in complete control. Many Christians in our world would prefer to belong to a kingdom that rules and dominates on a national and global scale rather than one that seeks to serve others.

The kingdom (or kin-dom) of God is surprising not only because it is marked by weakness and vulnerability but also because it's meant *for all.* It is nurtured, watered, and kneaded, to become something like a tree in which birds can find shelter or bread that nourishes entire communities. The kin-dom of God is a kin-dom of mutual flourishing. You work at it and invest in it like dough and like seeds so that in turn—and in its own time—it can nourish and serve others.

This is the power that the kin-dom of God holds: a power rooted in reciprocity.

"Let the earth grow plant life" says Genesis 1:11, "plants yielding seeds and fruit trees bearing fruit with seeds inside it." Throughout the creation narrative, the earth is described as a self-perpetuating "system of fertility and fruitfulness that provides for all."[3] Viewing creation not as a resource but as a life-sustaining force encourages us to serve it with gratitude for how it serves us.

This is why *all* things, not just fellow humans but the earth and all her inhabitants, should be seen as neighbor and kin. When we look at all created things with a sense of mutuality—an openness to give and to receive—we participate in the sacred.

●··●··●

I decided to finally visit the infested compost bin again after neglecting it for several weeks. When I opened the lid this time, the maggots were gone, and I found myself marveling at the cycle of life. I looked with wonder at the shape the banana peel had taken, how it was becoming one with the earth. The maggots had accomplished their task, breaking down the food waste so it would turn into the soil that will be used to shelter seeds as they grow into the food that will eventually decorate my dinner table and nourish my body. The food I eat will then become the milk that will feed and sustain my daughter as she suckles from my breast. Life, like the kingdom of God, is a beautiful and powerful ring of reciprocity—a *kin-dom* of mutual flourishing and nurturing.

"Cultures of gratitude must also be cultures of reciprocity," proclaims Robin Wall Kimmerer. She writes that all beings have a duty to one another. "An integral part of a human's education is to know those duties and how to perform them."[4] It is our calling to be stewards of our world: to know how to carry out the duties (and there are a myriad of them) that nurture and sustain all living things around us—from watering a garden to advocating for the rights of our marginalized neighbors.

Maybe next time I open my compost bin and see my slimy little friends, I'll whisper a "thank you" for the role they play in this wheel of life in which all created things have a purpose.

If I were recasting the message of the parable of the mustard seed into a parable of my own, I'd say something like this: the kingdom of God is like a tiny maggot that breaks down food waste into soil, which is used to plant a giant jack tree that grows fruit so large it feeds an entire neighborhood for a year.

The image of God's kin-dom as a maggot might make us squirm or scratch our heads, but maybe that's the point.

- What are the duties you feel called to participate in—both big and small?
- In what ways has God's reciprocal kingdom surprised you?

Day 8

Earth, Wind, Fire, Water

Streams came up from the earth and watered the whole surface
of the ground. Then the LORD God formed a man from the dust
of the ground and breathed into his nostrils the breath of life,
and the man became a living being.

—Genesis 2:6–7 (NIV)

The Gospel of John tells the story of a religious leader named Nicodemus who visits Jesus during the night. I imagine Nicodemus unable to sleep, tossing and turning, questions swirling in his head about
miracles and signs and teachings about God. He sneaks out of his
home under the light of the moon and listens to Jesus tell him about
what it means to be born of the Spirit. A cool breeze rattles the leaves,
blowing through the window. Jesus asks Nicodemus if he can feel the
wind blowing, and Nicodemus nods affirmatively. Jesus tells him that
this is what the Spirit of God is like.[1]

The next morning, Jesus continues through Judea, where people
are being baptized in the water by John, and then goes through Sa-
maria, where he meets a woman at a well in the middle of the day. The
sun is scorching, beating down on them. They are both exhausted. This
encounter is starkly different than the night before. This conversation
takes place in public with a woman on the margins rather than in secret
with a respected religious leader. Jesus tells her he is living water, and
she wonders what he means. He explains that whoever drinks of this
water will never be thirsty again.[2]

• • • • • • •

Growing up in a tropical landscape, I understood what wind and
water fused together in fury could do; they can destroy homes, hopes,

37

and lives. Living in California, I saw what hell a fire could bring when thousands of acres burned into dust, disintegrating plants and killing animals. I've felt the rumble of the earth beneath me, warning me that all could be toppled over in an instant—turning buildings into rubble and ocean waves into walls of ruin.

Power can devastate and destroy, but power can also liberate. Like other forces seen and unseen, where there is power to take and kill, there is also power to give and create, to sustain and energize.

Throughout much of history, the four basic elements—earth, wind, fire, and water—were the cornerstone of philosophy, science, and medicine, representing the foundational elements of the material world. They've also been used to describe the spiritual and mystical. From ancient civilizations to the modern day, the four sacred elements have represented the different energy forces in our world. For this reason, many Indigenous and Eastern cultures, traced all the way back to the Greeks in the fifth century BC, have made a practice of honoring the elements. Theologian Christine Valters Paintner notes that the ancient teachers "found a *symbolic* quality in each of the elements that expresses something none of the others could," a unique way of understanding the sacred.[3]

While modern Christianity hasn't generally revered the elements the way other cultures have, the Bible is saturated with this imagery for describing the divine. From a bush on fire in the wilderness to a gust of wind as described in John, Spirit consistently manifests through the basic elements of nature, reminding us that honoring them connects us to the natural world.

Thomas Merton once called the fields, the rain, the sun, the mud, and the wind our spiritual directors: "They form our contemplation. They instill us with virtue. They make us as stable as the land we live in."[4] Reflecting on the elements might open our hearts to new ways of engaging our spirituality and experiencing the divine.

Earth has often represented stability and nourishment, possessing a grounding quality that connects us to the physical. The earth relates to materiality—our roots and the foundation of life. From the Tree of Life to stories and images of feasting and food, the earth saturates Scripture, grounding and rooting us to that which sustains us.

Like the word "human," *humility* also comes from the root word *humus*, which means "earth." To be humble is to know our place, to be in touch with our origins from the dust of this earth. Humility means recognizing and understanding both our limits and our gifts intimately. It is only when we are deeply rooted to our bodies and to the earth that we can have a holistic relationship to God and to each other.

In the Bible, God is often described as a rock (see, e.g., Ps. 18:2). In the ancient world, rocks were valuable; they provided shelter and were used as building blocks and ornaments. Similarly, mountains and hills are referred to more often than any other geographical feature in the Bible. In fact, mountains are often places of encounter with the holy—such as Mount Sinai, where Moses meets God, and Mount Tabor, the site of Jesus's transfiguration. From Noah's ark planted atop a mountain to Jesus retreating to the Mount of Olives to pray, mountains are places of grounding and calling.[5]

Air or *wind* represents freedom, breath, sustenance, and wisdom. While invisible, wind enlivens everything. Air sustains us through the oxygen we draw into our lungs. Through soundwaves, it allows us to use our voices to speak, to communicate, and to sing.

Wind is a powerful force in Scripture, present at the beginning of creation and used as a metaphor for Spirit. In both Hebrew and Greek, the same word for "wind" can also mean "spirit" or "breath," depending on the context. Thus, Spirit encompasses all of these: air, wind, breath, and life. The Gospel of John affirms that wind can be heard but not seen—its movement dynamic and changeable, reminding us that God's ways are beyond our own. It is through the image of wind that God invites us into sacred mystery. It is also through the four winds that God breathes the breath of life into dry bones, bringing them to life (Ezek. 37:4–10).

Fire is about transformation, representing light, love, and passion. In Exodus, fire is a guide. Spirit manifests first in a burning bush (3:2); then again as a flame to lead the Israelites across the desert by night (13:21); and at Pentecost, when Spirit descended on the people and fire rested on each of them (Acts 2:3). Enlivened with Spirit, God's people are called "the light of the world" (Matt. 5:14), and when Jesus speaks to his disciples on the road to Emmaus, it causes them to feel as though their hearts were burning within them (Luke

24:32)—a common description for the feeling of illumination and enlightenment within one's soul.

Water represents nurturing, healing, rebirth, and clarity. In the first creation story in Genesis, water existed before everything else and is abundant on the earth. Water changes shape and form without losing its own nature, existing as ice, fluid, and steam.

Not only is the earth made up of water but so are our bodies. We are utterly dependent on water, as we drink it, absorb it, wash with it, and are cleansed by it. In our bodies, water carries oxygen and nutrients through our blood, aiding our bodies in producing serotonin, and getting rid of waste, toxins, oxidants, and positive ions, which can make the body ill in excessive amounts.

Water has served as a dominant symbol in religious practices. From Jewish *mikvahs* (ritual baths) for purification, to Christian baptisms, being submerged in water represents cleansing and rebirth. Prior to beginning his own ministry Jesus submerged himself in water, and it was through this process that the Spirit descended on him like a dove.

Jesus called himself living water, beckoning the thirsty to take a drink. But we don't just drink; we ourselves emanate this flow of living water (John 7:38).

●··●··●

Earth, wind, fire, and water are found at the heart of Scripture. The psalms, among other texts, include images and metaphors of each element to capture God's nature. And like anything that God chooses to reveal Godself through, the elements pulse with potential; they beam with lessons and teaching opportunities. But perhaps even more meaningful is the reality that when we engage in a relationship to the elements, we invite a deeper connection with the sacred. We find new ways of encountering the unique aspects of how divinity is manifested in the world.

If I ever want to feel whole again, I light my velita (candle) and watch how it illuminates the room, the smoke rising up alongside my prayers; or I let the earth cushion my body, sending sacred energy through her, speaking to me the things of heaven; or I feel the breeze blowing through my hair, connecting me to the Spirit of God; or I dig my toes into the sand at the edge of the ocean as the waves flow to and away from me.

These simple yet intentional practices ground me, connecting me deeper to God and to myself. Paintner writes that the elements are within us: "Our bodies are of the earth, our blood flows through us like water, air sustains our breath, and we are enlivened by the fire of the spirit in our own souls." They speak across traditions, rooting us through time and space in kinship with our ancestors who also looked to them as containers of sacred wisdom.[6]

- How might you honor the elements within you and outside of you?
- What are some ways that you can incorporate earth, wind, fire, and water into your daily life as a spiritual practice and reminder of the power and presence of the Spirit?

SPIRIT

Day 9

Ghost Stories

Very early in the morning, [Jesus] came to them, walking on the lake. He intended to pass by them.

—Mark 6:48

I once lived in a house that we thought was haunted. It was a small townhouse tucked away in a cul-de-sac on Calle Ocho. As soon as we moved in, our cats began scurrying about hissing at nothing, rolling on their backs and wailing as if they'd been attacked. It got so bad that we took Muka to the pet ER thinking she was sick, only for the vet to tell us she was "being dramatic." He put her on antidepressants and sent her home.

One day my little brother, barely seven years old, woke up from a nap on the couch and asked, "Who's that family standing by the door?"

We assured him there was no family standing by the door.

"Yes, there is. Right there. They're looking at me."

We saw nothing.

For months, we heard what sounded like scratches on the wall. One night I heard them in my bedroom. I knocked on the wall. It scratched back.

To this day, Mom swears that a bottle of pills was thrown at her while she was standing in the hallway. My stepdad still scoffs. "You saw those pills sprawled all over the floor, didn't you?" she demands, annoyed.

He admits he did see the pills thrown all over the floor.

Three Men and a Baby was a popular comedy released in 1987 about a New York City bachelor trio who raise a baby girl after she's left at their doorstep. In one scene of the movie, a ghostly figure of a little boy stands in the background by the window. For years, rumors spread that the figure was the ghost of a boy who had lived in the apartment. Apparently, he fell out the window and died just before filming began.

This legend boosted sales, and many people—including my family—found themselves standing in line at Blockbuster hoping to rent the movie and catch a glimpse of the ghost-boy. It turns out the rumor wasn't true; the ghostly figure was a cardboard cutout of one of the actors. I did not learn this until recently. I laid awake for years as a kid, staring at the window in my room, terrified that the ghost-boy might make his way from New York City to Miami.

Even skeptics (of which there are many) cannot deny that ghost stories do something in us and to us. They force us to grapple with our certainties: what we think we know about life, death, and the spiritual realm. Although we might doubt them, ghost stories still open up possibilities for how we understand reality, offering us the potential to expand our world and shift our perspectives.

● ● ● ● ● ●

Ghosts have been haunting humanity from the earliest days. Consulting with and believing in the spirit world were part of ancient Near Eastern culture at large. From the Israelites to the Egyptians to the Mesopotamians to the Canaanites and then the Greeks, the ancient world had a rich ghost culture. As Sze-kar Wan writes, "The line between the living and the dead was fluid and porous."[1] It was a common Jewish belief that the spirit of a person was not at rest until they were buried properly. Amulets used to ward off spirits have been found at the burial sites of ancient Israelites.

Ghosts are present in the Talmud and medieval Jewish literature. The Bible itself is no stranger to the paranormal. In Deuteronomy 18:11, for example, God tells the Israelite people not to associate with those who conjure spirits—implying that the living can indeed communicate with the dead. However, Jewish scholars argue that this wasn't for any ethical or theological reason. The purpose of this prohibition was to keep the Israelites as distinct from all other peoples.[2] Some also argue that this instruction was rooted in the notion that God's people weren't to pay too much attention to the dead, lest they ignore the living.[3]

There's one popular ghost story in the Bible that's worthy of consideration. It happens right after the feeding of the five thousand in Mark, when the disciples get into a boat to head across the lake. During the night, the wind becomes violent and terrorizes them. In the midst of the chaos, the disciples see Jesus walking on water, and they think he is a ghost (Mark 6:49).[4] I find this detail intriguing—an invitation into the great mystery of the spiritual world.

Commentators point out the particular timing of this event. Since it happened just after the feeding of multitudes, they say, it speaks to the cluelessness of the disciples. After witnessing this miracle, they *should* have recognized Jesus's divinity. But if we keep reading, we see that Jesus wasn't particularly concerned with the *should*. As always, Jesus was more interested in meeting people in their doubts than in bolstering their perceived certainties.

The Bible says that Jesus came to them walking on the lake, but "he intended to pass by them" (Mark 6:48). Have you ever noticed that last part? It leaves me with questions. First of all, where was Jesus going? Did he start walking toward them but then get distracted? Was he intending to pass by them with a different destination in view? Did he have another place—another boat—he was looking to go to?

Jesus was headed *somewhere* in the middle of the lake, and it *wasn't* toward his disciples. At least initially. And it seems it wasn't until after they saw him and cried out in fear that Jesus decided to redirect—to change course from walking toward *something* to walking toward *them*.

"Take courage! It is I. Do not be afraid," he said (6:50 NIV).

Then he got into the boat with them.

I'm left to wonder: If the disciples had known this was Jesus, would he have had reason to get in the boat with them? Would he have kept walking toward whatever he was walking toward had they recognized him? Would he have gone to them if they had been certain of who he was?

There's really no way of knowing, but pondering these questions makes me think that maybe it's not our doubt that positions us away from Jesus but rather our certainty.

And maybe—sometimes—those doubts can serve as saving graces.

Flannery O'Connor once said that "even in the life of a Christian, faith rises and falls like the tides of an invisible sea."[5] I think about this often, about how the low tides of our lives can make us feel stranded and alone. Our faith may be so battered by the violent winds of life that it might leave us feeling the same way the disciples did: unsure and afraid. But sometimes we squint in the dark of the night, when our faith is at a low point, and find Jesus headed our way—ready to get into the boat with us at the first sound of our cries.

God is not surprised, intimidated, disappointed, or offended by what makes us human. We are loved when the tide is high and when it is low.

We often use words like *immutable* and *omniscient* to describe a God who is unchanging and all-knowing, and while these things may be true, this story tells me something else is true: the Spirit of God is a spirit who redirects—even and especially when we are uncertain, doubtful, or afraid.

And despite the disciples' fears that this guy they spent most of their time with was a *ghost*, Jesus heard them and responded. He loved them and comforted them and met them in that place where they were—in the middle of a storm in the middle of nowhere—and I like to think that's exactly what Spirit still does. Sometimes I wonder if maybe Jesus felt their confusion offered a good opportunity to teach them something. Perhaps this encouraged them to keep grappling with what they *thought* they knew about him, about life, and even about death.

When it comes to a life of faith, we're often haunted with preconceived ideas of the divine and are left with a spirituality that is stunted and therefore cannot grow. But if we remain open to possibility, like the disciples, we might be met with a God who is alive, dynamic, one who changes course in order to comfort us.

●··●··●

By the time these words are published, I will have completed almost eight years of formal theological education at the graduate level, requiring me to have read many thousands of pages from scores of books and articles. I'll have learned the biblical languages and written nearly a hundred academic papers (or at least it feels like it), and after all this, more than anything, I am convinced that the words *I don't know* are a sacred declaration.

I used to be really sure about a lot of things. My faith depended on my certainty that I had all the right answers to all the big questions. But now? Well, now, one of the few things I'm sure of is that the Spirit of God doesn't need us to be sure at all before getting into the boat with us.

Day 10

What Do You Want?

❧

Turning around, Jesus saw them following and asked, "What do you want?"

—John 1:38 (NIV)

I often wonder what God sounds like.

"I heard you in the garden," Adam told God after he ate the fruit and then tried to hide (Gen. 3:10 NIV). What did he hear? Was it the quiver of leaves on trees? The crunch of earth beneath soles of feet? Much about the divine is left to the reader's imagination, and while this might frustrate some, I think it's a precious gift—to be given the freedom to dream and to imagine. Perhaps God invites us to wonder so that something unexpected might be awakened in us.

There's a story in 1 Kings in which Elijah spends the night at Mount Horeb. While he's there, God says to wait for him, as he's going to pass by. First, a "very strong wind" rips through the mountains and breaks apart the stones. Surely that was God. "But the LORD wasn't in the wind." Immediately following the wind is an earthquake. Elijah thinks surely *that* was God. "But the LORD wasn't in the earthquake" (19:11). After the earthquake, there's a fire. You guessed it; God wasn't in the fire either.

This story intrigues me because it seems like God is playing tricks on Elijah, testing him, as many claim God often does. God knew Elijah was expecting him, so why would he send the elements with such fury, only to not appear in them? Then the text says, "After the fire there was a sound. Thin. Quiet" (19:12).

When Elijah heard this, he wrapped his face in his coat—speechless, I imagine, something beautiful stirring inside of him.

It couldn't be.

It was.

I would give anything to hear what Elijah heard. Was it a sound at all? Did Elijah hear it outside himself or from within?

●··●··●

Dominant culture has long convinced us that the voice of God sounds like a white man with a Bible and a pulpit—thunderous, furious, loud—telling us what not to believe, who not to love, who not to be. We've been bombarded with loud messages about all we ought not to be, all the while drowning out the thin and quiet, still and small—the gentle whisper within us we've been trained to ignore—that speaks to us about all that we are.

A friend once said that figuring out the will of God in our lives is not like some cosmic pursuit but more like an afternoon at the playground. Instead of us hounding God as if we are in a frantic cartoon chase, we find God patient, sitting on a bench, pleased to observe our antics. We might want to slide down the slide, but we are unsure. We may be nervous that this piece of equipment is off-limits. We might ask if it's okay.

"Of course, go ahead," God assures us. Then we might want to swing on the monkey bars. Worried we might not be allowed, we might pause, look over at God and ask, "Can I swing on the monkey bars?" God will walk over and remind us: "Yes, this playground is a safe space for you. You are free to slide or swing or sit."

It's up to you, what do you want to do?

I quite like this analogy. I remember how nervous I often was to make a wrong decision. What if I picked the wrong school to attend, the wrong apartment to move into? What if I missed God's will because I didn't pray long or hard enough? Figuring out God's will felt like an impossible Easter egg hunt in which all the eggs were painted the color of dirt and buried underground.

I know I'm not alone in this. Many of us have trouble discerning what we want, or we might be afraid to make our own choices because we were taught to distrust our own voices. The "genuine" in ourselves may not seem to align with the dominant culture's brand of Christianity, or we may feel crushed under the weight of a scarcity mindset. In many ways we've confused the sound of the divine with that of guilt, shame, judgment. We've been told to disregard our wants, ignore our desires.

But what if Jesus offers another way: inviting folks to know and understand these longings?

In John's Gospel, he tells the story of two men who were disciples of John the Baptist. They see Jesus walking by, and John the Baptist tells them that this man Jesus is the lamb of God. So the two men decide to follow Jesus. "What do you want?" Jesus asks when he notices them (John 1:38 NIV). I admit, I spent so much of my Christian life wondering what God wanted from me that I rarely stopped to think about what I wanted. And I never once noticed Jesus asking this question to anyone either.

But this isn't the only time he asks something akin to this.

"What do you want me to do for you?" Jesus asks two men who beg him to have mercy on them (Matt. 20:32). Didn't Jesus know what they wanted? But that wasn't of interest to Jesus. It seems what interested him is that they knew what they wanted for themselves.

I wonder if in asking these questions Jesus was trying to relay something I now know to be true: being attuned to what it is that I want is key to living fully into "God's will" for my life.

What are you drawn to?

What moves you?

What brings you joy?

What breaks your heart?

Who are you?

Knowing the answer to these questions offers a path toward healing and liberation, not just individually but for our collective whole—so that we may better love and care for ourselves and each other.

Later in Jesus's ministry, he comes across a man possessed by demons. This man, isolated from community, is living among tombs, crying out and harming himself with stones. He runs out to see Jesus.

"What's your name?" Jesus asks him (Luke 8:30). We tend to think Jesus's question is for the demons, but I wonder if he really was asking the man. Perhaps he wants to know who this man is. About this Howard Thurman says, "For a moment [the possessed man's] tilted mind righted itself and he said, 'That's it, I don't know, there are legions of me. And they riot in my streets. If I only knew, then I would be whole.'"[1] For Thurman, these two questions—*Who are you?* and *What do you want?*—are key to hearing "the sound of the genuine" in you, because failure to discern this subjects us to spending the rest of our lives "on the ends of strings that somebody else pulls."[2] To know who we really are, to know what we really want, is to hear the voice of God within ourselves. It is to be so in tune with our Creator that we can feel free to slide or climb or sit and trust we are known and loved and held.

I think back to the story of Elijah and how he expected to hear God in the loud, in the thunderous, in the ways we're told God speaks. We sometimes have been listening to the voices of others for so long that we've mistaken them for our own. But it was in the thin and gentle whisper where God's voice could be found—that quiet voice within, speaking the truths we've always longed to hear. If only we might learn to listen.

Our innermost selves "have unknown terrains," writes Puerto Rican theologian Lisa Colón DeLay. Yet so often our inner worlds remain unexplored. This expanse—this "wild land within," as she calls it—includes every part of ourselves, from our minds and spirits to our aspirations and memories. We know very little about our innermost selves, often due to the "commotion of our lives."[3]

The outer world distracts us from paying attention to our innermost self, telling us to seek answers instead of "listening to the questions," as Henri Nouwen notes.[4] But our innermost selves are worthy of our attention. They are worthy of familiarity and love, for if we know who we are on the inside, no one can ever define us—or the divine within us—from the outside.

- Who are you?
- What do you want?

Native Conversations

🌱

In the beginning was the Word
and the Word was with God
and the Word was God.

—John 1:1

When I was young, I believed that every language had an English and a Spanish version. After my elementary school teacher taught us a few words in Mandarin, I raised my hand to ask if what we just learned was the English or the Spanish version of the language. Confused, she told me it was just Mandarin. I figured that meant it was the Spanish version, as that was my primary language.

For me, language was both infinite and intimate. As a bilingual kid, there were sentiments, expressions, and even people I identified strictly with one language or the other. For instance, I believed that every abuela on the planet spoke only Spanish. When I met my first English-speaking grandmother in my twenties, my world exploded.

Language has always had a sacred nature about it. Words have been the bearers of worlds, holding within them a multiplicity of meanings. Strung together, black marks on a white page stir something unique in us, igniting our souls, and whispering to us secrets we've always longed to hear. They can make us sweat, cry, laugh; they can be smelled and tasted, heard and felt.

The first time I read John 1:1 in English, it captivated me: "In the beginning was the *Word*." Few descriptions of Jesus stand out so powerfully—particularly because of my love for words. Growing up with Spanish as my first language, however, I understood John 1:1 quite differently. The version I became familiar with reads: "En el principio ya existía el Verbo," which translates to, "In the beginning already existed the Verb."[1] Jesus, *the Verb of God. The action of God.* This is the image of Jesus I knew from a young age.

The difference in translation speaks to the power that language holds—how la Espíritu Santa (the Holy Spirit) makes herself known to differing groups of people in unique ways. Jesus is a word and a verb: a transcendent picture of both the mystery of God and the expansive nature of Scripture. But more than just a single word, or even a verb, is an entire conversation.

In her book *Church of the Wild*, Victoria Loorz explains that the Greek word *logos* (translated as "word" in English) was first used in reference to cosmology to conceptualize the relationship between all things. Later, the Greeks used *logos* to describe this relationship between all things as a sacred or divine process of dialogue.[2] Perhaps *this* is what John had in mind when he penned his Gospel: Christ the *logos*, the *conversation.*

Language is beautiful. Language also bears weight. Words don't just communicate; they shape culture, identity, and even our emotions. They're our portal to meaning-making, connection, healing, learning, and self-awareness.[3]

In the same way, my world continued to shift as I read the Bible in its original languages. Each new vocabulary word carried with it a detonator: how "compassion" comes from "womb," how there are five different words for "cow," or the fact that the name Adam simply means "earth creature."

One word worth noting in our modern context is the one often translated in the New Testament as "righteousness." The Greek transliteration is *dikaiosunē*, which is also the word for "justice." This is important to note, as in Western Christianity these two words imply very different meanings. Righteousness often relates to personal piety, and justice refers to how we engage others on a societal level. If we used "justice" in place of "righteousness" where the context suits it, many of the passages we're familiar with would read very differently. For example, what if we read Matthew 5:6 as "Blessed are those who hunger and thirst for *justice*, for they will be filled"?

The Bible is such a powerful tool—both for good and for evil—because it is a book of words: authoritative, sacred words written in languages not our own, translated and interpreted so that we may understand and apply its principles timelessly.

Like many other things, however, a lot gets lost in translation.[4]

Throughout history, language has been used to perpetuate domination and power. Native tongues spoken by native bodies are deemed inferior by invaders bent on conquering and taking control. Dominant voices spin language in order to make the narrative favorable to their viewpoint. But to speak a native tongue is to speak intimacy and mystery. It is to speak the language of God.

This is why the belief that the Bible, with its miracles and resurrections and a God who communicates through wind and fire, is "plain and clear" is so dangerous. Such belief can strip it of its healing power—its mystery and wonder—similar to what folks do when they interpret "the Word" in John 1:1 as the Bible itself instead of Jesus. This makes sense, however, when we've been taught to fear mystery, to fear what we cannot understand. A God who cannot be contained by one language or one culture or one way of being in the world is frightening. It means we could be wrong about God, and there's too much resting on being right.

This is part of what makes Pentecost so powerful. In Acts 2, the moment Spirit arrives on the scene, pandemonium ensues: wind and fire swirl throughout the house like a tornado—loud and violent. What fascinates me is that *the* marker of divine presence is people speaking in their "native languages" (2:6). *This* is how the revolution begins, "the revolution of the intimate," as Willie James Jennings calls it.[5] The full presence of Spirit is alive through words: words being spoken aloud in the midst of the mayhem, where ears strain to hear, tuning into familiar sounds, into language infinite and intimate. "To speak a language is to speak a people." It is to speak "familiarity, connection, and relationality."[6]

In the beginning was the Conversation, a "relationship-between" that bound the cosmos together. In an action that extended far beyond that first Pentecost, the Spirit ushered in a deep tetheredness—a binding held together by the intimate back and forth of native languages in dialogue.

Day 12

Lingering in the Tension

❧

At that the boy's father cried out, "I have faith; help my lack of faith!"

—Mark 9:24

You know those last few weeks before spring, when winter is trying desperately to hold on, her bony fingers cold and frail, losing their grip to the warmth of the sun? The trees towering above your head might still be bare, but when you look down, buds of purple are sprinkled across the ground, bursting forth from earth's womb.

It's March as I write this, that interstitial month lodged between the dry chill of February and the damp warmth of April. Yesterday I took my dogs out around noon. It was sixty degrees. The sun was shining, and I was sporting a T-shirt. Today I woke up to a gray sky, below freezing temperatures, and three inches of snow.

Emily Freeman once said about these strange days: "It's the season of the in-between, surrounded by many opposing true things, when nature sends us quiet reminders to hold the tension longer."[1] If we pay close attention, we might notice the earth constantly beckoning us to receive this gift. On bended knees with cool breath and a warm touch, the natural world asks us to stay in this moment. *Right here. A little longer.*

Do you feel it?

●‑●‑●‑●

Isn't it curious that right before Jesus raised Lazarus from the dead, he cried?

When Lazarus's sister Mary threw herself at Jesus's feet in anger and in grief, chastising his delay in arriving to see them, Jesus didn't defend himself. He didn't reprimand her forwardness either. Instead, he let her grief find a home with him, hot tears dripping down both their faces. Have you ever wondered why Jesus wept when he knew Lazarus would be resurrected? Upon seeing Mary's sorrow, "He was deeply moved in spirit and troubled" (John 11:33). Without offering platitudes or silver linings, Jesus let the sadness linger as long as was necessary. In that moment, a friend and a brother was dead, and the only appropriate response was to cry.

The life and death of Jesus offers an invitation to sit in a sacred tension, but many are not comfortable doing this. We are a people hell-bent on fix-its, uncomfortable with struggle or with sadness. Perhaps this is why, for many of us, Holy Saturday has long been ignored. This is the day between the death of Christ on Good Friday and his resurrection on Easter Sunday. In the immigrant Catholic church I attended with abuela growing up, this holy day of waiting was as important as Easter Sunday because it mirrored our reality—the constant push and pull between sorrow and joy, death and resurrection. On this day, we lit velas (candles) and sat in front of the altar for what felt like years. We knew joy would come, but there was no rush. The holy tension was a space in which we felt most alive. I didn't know it back then, but la Espíritu Santa was forming something sacred in me.

Perhaps this is why I'm so drawn to the father in Mark 9 who begs Jesus to save his son from the demon that had possessed him. Jesus tells him that all things are possible for one who has faith. "I have faith; help my lack of faith," says the father (9:24). Notice he says he both has faith and lacks it. Some days his faith seemed perfectly fine, I'm sure. But what about those times of uncertainty I suspect we all feel now and then? Just moments before his encounter with Jesus, the apostles tried to heal his son, but they couldn't. What about the lack of faith that inevitably came in that moment? What the father articulated to Jesus was a deep truth that is often only known in struggle: the spiritual life is one lived in between belief and nonbelief, faith and lack of faith at the same time. Perhaps our liberation is found in our ability to linger well in that tension.

●··●··●

I spiraled into a sadness the first few months that COVID-19 began ripping through our communities and robbing us of our neighbors and our perceived freedoms.

Right before stay-at-home orders were put in place in Los Angeles, Taylor and I walked to a restaurant a few minutes down the road from our apartment. When we bid the owners farewell after our meal, we promised we'd be back soon. We didn't comprehend the gravity of what was to come. A couple weeks later, after LA was shut down, we walked past the same restaurant and noticed a note on the door written to the community: "Thank you for 12 great years. We love you." I couldn't hold back my tears for the remainder of our walk home. I allowed the grief of our collective experience to wash over me.

Life felt particularly uncertain and scary those early months of the pandemic. Notifications flooded my phone with rising death tolls. Hospitals turned sick patients away. Our Asian siblings endured racist slurs, fighting hatred that needed someone to blame. We waited for hours in lines at depleted grocery stores with limits on how many could enter, donning gloves and scarves as shields.

Taylor had recently started a new job, one that had given us just enough financial security to breathe a little easier and start freeing ourselves from the burden of student debt. A few days after quarantine began, his pay was cut—leaving us with an added layer of anxiety over the future. I know we weren't alone in this.

It was all too much to bear. I soon stopped answering my phone and then stopped getting out of bed in the mornings. Fear closed in on me, and the suggestions for coping that came from those who sought to draw me out of my cocoon only made me feel more stuck inside of it. Family and friends tried to put a positive spin on things: "Why don't you go for a walk, practice gratitude, or cook something new?" "Well, at least he wasn't let go completely," they'd tell me.

I know they had good intentions, but silver linings only poisoned me with anger. I could go for a walk or cook something new, but that wouldn't rid me of the grief over the rising death count. I could be grateful for the job my husband still had while also feeling scared as hell about what the pay cut could mean. These opposing things were both true at the same time.

Besides, didn't everything we were experiencing as a global community, a collective people, warrant my sadness? Why would I want to pretend it wasn't happening? The world was so heavy; the very least I could do was honor that. Katherine May writes about sadness in her book *Wintering*, "[It] is one of the simple things in life: a pure, basic emotion to be respected, if not savored." Sadness is instructive. It has a function, she explains; it tells us that something is going wrong.[2]

The only thing that felt right was resisting the "Well, at least ..." refrain of the privileged and choosing to let the Jesus who weeps and Spirit who sighs linger with me a little longer. May continues, "Sometimes the best response to our howls of anguish is the honest one. We need friends who wince along with our pain, who tolerate our gloom, and who allow us to be weak for a while, while we're finding our feet again. We need people who acknowledge that we can't always hang on. That sometimes everything breaks."[3] It's nothing short of wholly glorious that Jesus was precisely that friend.

It was in the lingering that I realized something: this *was* my silver lining. My silver lining was the very act of giving myself the opportunity to remain tender for as long as I needed to. My silver lining was not rushing past Good Friday, because to grieve is to be human, and I will not sacrifice my humanity at the altar of positivity. I didn't need to feel better. I just needed to feel alive. I just needed to feel human.

My father-in-law died a few short months before my daughter was born. Hours after her birth, my husband and I lay together in bed, our baby resting on my chest, her skin still coated in thick, white vernix. I was still buzzing, high from exhaustion and adrenaline, still in shock at what my body had done. We were both processing the reality that our lives had just changed. "We are parents," we whispered to each other.

We spent the next few hours sending pictures to Abuela and Grandma, responding to congratulations, and taking selfies with our tiny human while tears rolled off our cheeks. It was a moment that defined all moments. *We are parents.*

Taylor looked at me, and his gaze turned heavy: "I wish I could send him a picture of her."

"I wish you could too," I told him. Our hearts were torn in two. We lingered, tethered to a grief and to a joy beyond words, and we had never felt more alive, more human, than we did in that tender moment. *Right here. A little longer.*

- What moments of sacred tension stand out in your life? What did they speak to you about your humanity?
- What might Jesus's response to Mary at Lazarus's death teach us about lingering and about connecting with one another?

Day 13

Arguing with God

❧

"Come now, and let's settle this,"
says the Lord.
—Isaiah 1:18

I sat across from my seminary's beloved New Testament professor at an Irish pub with colleagues and friends, smacking my palm on the table in jest every time I thought I made a good point. I was arguing with an expert on Paul, about Paul, while more than a dozen peering eyeballs watched us like a ping-pong match. I don't remember what we were going on about. I knew I was probably wrong about whatever I pretended to be so sure about, but it didn't matter. I was having fun, and best of all, I was learning—holding all my opinions in an open hand, willing to let them be changed.

I don't care about arguing over Paul anymore, even if just for fun. I don't think he would want that anyway. He'd probably pen us an angry letter if he knew what an idol the church has made of him and how his words have been misused to oppress others in the name of God.

In my first book, *Abuelita Faith*, I write about how confrontation is intimacy, about how I learned that at the domino table. Those nights when as a young girl I sat on laps, watching wide-eyed as family members squabbled across their fichas (domino tiles), were holy preparations, dress rehearsals for the moments in life I'd have to stand up for myself and assert my own dignity. This was something I would eventually need to do when I came up against injustices perpetrated with the aim to silence and control.

Fast-forward to a time several years down the road, when I found myself sitting at another table, in a context where a pastor refused to affirm my full humanity as a Cuban woman leader in the church.

I was nervous walking into the coffee shop, my heart in my throat. The insecurities that came with the messages I'd internalized about my "role" and my "place" as a woman plagued me. But a confidence would sweep over me. Not a confidence in my own abilities but a certainty that came solely from clinging to my truth, which in this case, I believed, was aligned with Spirit's.

The pastor I was meeting with had been telling congregants that I was "unsubmissive" because I had gathered with other women in the church to read the Bible without asking his permission. I opened my Bible to Matthew 28, and slammed it on the table, and in front of the other patrons, exclaimed: "All authority has been given to Jesus, not you!" I will not apologize for disrupting their morning. It was a turning point of sorts; this was the day I'd first be empowered by Spirit to begin challenging the wolves in shepherds' clothing.

Some might say that I shouldn't have questioned this pastor's authority, as doing so is equivalent to questioning and arguing with God: "Does the clay have any right to question the potter?" (see Isa. 45:9). How dare I argue with the divine or his appointed leaders?

But oftentimes, our voices are the key to our release from the restraints others try to put on us.

In the first chapter of Isaiah, God is angry at the Israelites for offering meaningless sacrifices and for failing to do the thing they were called to—namely, seek justice, help the oppressed, defend the orphan, plead for the widow.

For seventeen verses God lets the Israelites have it, and then suddenly the mood seems to shift. I imagine God pausing, perhaps giving something akin to a sigh and, with a tone of compassion, offering this invitation, "Come now, let's settle this" (Isa. 1:18). Translations vary from "Let's reason together" to "Let's argue it out" to "Let's discuss this."

This has quickly become one of my favorite verses. Regardless of the way it's translated, the message remains the same; despite what we may have heard from those in authority, God not only welcomes our disputes and challenges, God also invites us to weigh in. Even in anger, we are encouraged to state our cases, to argue it out.

●··●··●

Judaism is a tradition that has always encouraged engagement. The day-to-day of Jewish life is built not only on disagreement and argument but also on asking questions. "To be without questions is not a sign of faith, but a lack of depth."[1] To answer a question with a question is a common way folks engaged with one another and with the text, as challenging yourself to think more deeply is one of Judaism's central tenets. In fact, the name *Israel* literally means "wrestled with God." Argument with God is a particularly Jewish method of asking for proof of God's goodness in the presence of evil. Scholars call this a "law-court" style of prayer. Anson Laytner notes, "It is the Jewish mode of appealing to God the Chief Justice of the Supreme Court against God the Partner, and records of such protest/appeals may be found in the literature of practically every period of Jewish history."[2]

We see this in how Abraham argues with God over the fate of Sodom and Gomorrah, convincing God to spare the cities. We also see it with Moses, Elijah, Jeremiah, and Job—all of whom also questioned God, either on behalf of a third party or by arguing their personal case. The book of Lamentations as well as the psalms of lament go even further, portraying arguing with the divine as a form of prayer.[3]

But this is what I find most compelling: argument with God is always rooted in justice. "The question that echoes through the history of Judaism—from Abraham to Jeremiah to Job to rabbinic *midrash* to medieval lament—is not acceptance of, but protest against, injustice," writes Rabbi Jonathan Sacks.[4] In Scripture, the notion of arguing with God arises not from a desire to be right but as a response to the oppression the people endure.

If we follow a Jewish Jesus, with whom questions (and disagreements and arguments) were both common and expected, then why are so many Christians conditioned to feel guilty or shameful for having them? Perhaps the answer lies in the notion of power. The history of Christendom knows this well, as the church has historically held absolute power in civic life. This sentiment persists even in modern Protestant traditions in which pastors lord their authority over their congregations. Questioning and arguing with God, then, opens the door to questioning and arguing with those who have positions of power and expect others to defer to them. These god-men must preserve their *power-over* to continue exercising artificial and patriarchal spiritual hierarchy. This is how abusers have ravaged the church, maintaining their positions and incomes at the expense of our dignity and humanity. As Brené Brown writes about those who strive to exert power over others, "It's a desperate attempt to maintain a very fragile ego. It's the desperate scramble of self-worth quicksand." When people act this way, "they're showing us exactly what they're afraid of."[5]

But Jesus gave up power and privilege to stand in solidarity with humanity. In this way, the Spirit of God sets aside power-over in favor of *power-with* for the sake of justice. Where power-over is marked by dominance, coercion, and control, power-with is marked by collaboration and cocreation. It is a power rooted in collective action and relationship. A God who invites us to "argue it out" is a God of power-with, power shared. This God is dynamic: one who feels, who responds to our pleas, and who can be accessed by humans. This is a God many of us were not introduced to but had to discover on our own.

●··●··●

When was the last time you argued with the divine? The last time you stated your case, reasoned together? And what if the whole of Christian history had approached the Bible this way, not as a tool for silencing but as a means for exploration, deep dialogue, and faithful questioning that is sensitive to the nuances and complexities of life and faith? Where might we be if Scripture invited us into holy curiosity?

There are a lot of things I cannot be certain of, but I am certain that God is not fragile. Nor is God in the business of creating subjugated people with no liberty to question or to wonder. Arguing not only with God but also with God's sacred text is a path toward our liberation, a way of pushing back against the forces of injustice that plague us.

Humans are thinking and feeling creatures, passionate at times, and the Spirit of God invites all of that—all the critical thinking, all the deep engagement, all the reasoning together—into the relationship we have together. This intimacy, this authenticity, goes to the very heart of what it is to know and be known by Spirit.

If you can bare your angst, your frustrations, your disagreements, and your dread to someone, yet they are unshaken, what sort of healing and liberation might be found with this person? How much more so should this be true with the divine? To argue with God is to belong to God; it is to embrace a love that surpasses all understanding—and be transformed by it.

Day 14

The Gift of Dreams

Listen to my words: "When there is a prophet among you, I, the
LORD, reveal myself to them in visions, I speak to them in dreams."

—Numbers 12:6 (NIV)

"I had two dreams about someone I know being pregnant. It turns out one was the receptionist at the office, but I'm not sure who the other is," my mother told me.

I gulped my water. I was eight weeks pregnant and had yet to tell my family.

"Hm, that's weird," I said, not sure I sounded convincing.

For the last few decades, Mom has been able to sense through dreams every pregnancy in our family and community and in any workplace she's been in before the official announcement.

Mom has always had a fascination with dreams. And consequently, so have I. Throughout my childhood, I kept a pen and paper by my bed, jotting down my dreams as soon as I'd wake up so I wouldn't forget. I'd beg God to speak to me through them, wishing for a revelation like folks in the Bible.

This changed as I got older. I stopped paying attention to my dreams after I learned the physiological explanation for them; they are triggered by neurotransmitters in our brain replenished during REM sleep, resulting in an altered chemical state.[1] It's a shame that as adults, we learn to sacrifice our wonder at the altar of reason.

Scientists haven't reached consensus on the purpose of dreams. Some speculate that they help us to problem solve, find emotional balance, or think flexibly. Still others offer that they reveal unconscious desires, tap into our wiser selves, or mean nothing at all. My sense is that something otherworldly happens when we're dreaming, something that cannot be fully explained or understood. This is reason enough to pay attention.

Perhaps their mysterious nature is behind why dreams have often been seen as an avenue through which to connect more deeply with Spirit. In fact, our neglect of them in the modern world is a historical anomaly. Within communities throughout history, including ancient Israel, dreams and spirituality are intimately connected. Dreams occur when we're in a vulnerable state, thus opening us to the recognition that we are part of something larger. In Scripture, for example, they're places and portals of divine encounter.

More than twenty dreams are recorded in the Hebrew Scriptures and the New Testament. Some reveal divine plans; others portend the future. Some dreams are symbolic, and others are more straightforward. There are dreams that warn and others that give direction.

Dreams are described as one of the ongoing ways Spirit will manifest: "I will pour out my spirit upon everyone" the prophet Joel said, delivering God's words. "Your sons and your daughters will prophesy, your old men will dream dreams, and your young men will see visions" (Joel 2:28).

All people—even today—are able to experience the sacred through them.

● ● ● ● ● ● ●

Carl Jung was a leading psychologist on dreams and dream interpretation. Jung, raised in a traditional Christian home, experienced dreams that spoke specifically to the nuances of God's nature. As ridiculous as it sounds, he once had a dream about a turd falling from the throne of God, and it changed the course of his life.

Prior to his dream, Jung was gripped with fear of being sent to hell for believing things he was told were contrary to his faith. He interpreted this notable dream as grace, as it taught him the difference between a superficial faith of simply following the rules of tradition and an awakened, dynamic faith marked by obedience "to the living God as he experienced him."[2] Jung's dream transformed his relationship to God and influenced his psychoanalytic approach, allowing him to change countless lives through his work.

Dreams present images of the divine in new and unexpected ways, particularly during periods of spiritual confusion, crisis, and struggle. After years of mistreatment, Laban makes peace with his son-in-law Jacob through the direction given in a dream (Gen. 31:24). It is through dreams that the birth of Jesus as the Messiah is foretold (Matt. 1:21), and through a dream, Pontius Pilate's wife realizes Jesus is innocent during his trial (Matt. 27:19).

In the Bible and beyond, dreams have helped people find spiritual direction and access deeper states of awareness. The activity in our sleeping brain is similar to the type of activity that occurs when we pray or meditate. Just as we are more susceptible to recognize the Spirit speaking to us when we engage in these transcendent spiritual practices, maybe the same can be true when we dream.

Native cultures throughout history have believed that dreams reveal truth from ancestors, from guardian spirits, or from within. And in many cases, the awakened world is guided by the direction and insight received through dreams. Remembering and honoring dreams serves as a form of resistance and a way to preserve cultural heritage.[3] For many who have been marginalized by the dominant culture, the dream world represents the liminal space they inhabit—a space that reminds them of the mutability of their reality.

●•·●•·●

I once had a vivid dream about my abuelo (grandfather), who I never met. In the dream, I saw him playing with a young girl as she rode her red tricycle by an abandoned home. When I described the dream to Mom, tears flooded her eyes. She has a memory identical to it from her time in Cuba. Abuelo died while Mom was in her early teens; reminders of his traumatic death still sting. Remembering this memory was a sacred gift—one she'll always hold close.

Studies have shown that dreams help us cope with stress, grief, and trauma, bringing to light what is wounded or forgotten in us and in our world. They play an important role in some of our primary emotional and cognitive systems, showing us paths of remembrance, repair, and healing.[4] They've helped us solve problems and master skills we're working through in the waking world by reinforcing new pathways in our brain. Similarly, they help us become more self-aware, drawing deep-rooted anxieties and desires to the surface.[5] Layered with meaning and memories, dreams can offer a wisdom deeper and more accurate than our conscious thoughts.

I once heard a dreamworker say that we must have a cyclical view of dreams. While we are taught in the West to have a linear view of events, we must approach our dreams with patience and curiosity, seeing what might come back around over time. This is part of our healing work: it must be nurtured with care and patience.

More important than interpreting our dreams is witnessing them and recognizing their power. As Jill Hammer suggests, dreams are able to shift our realities in the waking world, serving as allies as we struggle for justice in this changing and challenging world.[6] But this requires our full participation.

While the art of sacred dreaming has been lost to many of us in the West, we can choose to recover it by returning to the dreaming practices of our ancestors. The culture we live in might try to disconnect us from the earth, from each other, and from our bodies, but "dreams show us another way."[7] To reconnect to the dreamworld is to look inward, and to be ready to listen to all the ways the Spirit might be engaging with us. And so perhaps this is what we can learn about our dreams: the practice of paying attention to what is seen and unseen. And in this, we might allow what *could be* to take root inside of us, so that we may be encouraged, inspired, and healed to take action.

"If we fail to take the simple steps to remember and understand our dreams, it is as though we are throwing away a gift from our brains without bothering to open it," writes Alice Robb.[8] What might it look like to receive the gifts available to us—even in our sleep?

- Are there any dreams that are meaningful to you? What gifts might these dreams be offering?
- Has your reality shifted through dreams? If so, in what way?

The Spirit Speaks

❦

"Speak. I'm listening."

—1 Samuel 3:10

(NIrV)

During my early twenties, I'd take summers off from teaching at a small private school to lead teams of adolescents and their chaperones on service projects in cities around the globe. Every other week I'd board a plane with my oversized backpack and land somewhere new: from Denver, Colorado, to Iquitos, Peru.

On one trip, after a missed flight and in desperate need of a bed, I found myself poking through the screen of a friend's house in Gainesville, Georgia, where the only light source was the moon and the only sounds I heard were those of the frogs stretching their throats in unison. My friend was off leading her own trip and told me that a window in her house didn't lock. I could sneak in, wash my clothes, sleep in her bed, and eat stale chips from her pantry. All of which I did.

The next day I made the eight-hour drive to my destination—a small church where we'd be lodging and doing some needed rehab work—through winding mountain roads without cell reception and with paper instructions taped to my dashboard that read, "You'll know you're there when you see a barn to your left and a gate held together by chains."

I stopped for a snack on my way through the small Appalachian town in West Virginia where I would be spending the next couple weeks, making sure to erase my Miami accent at the counter, drawing out my syllables like a fraud. With a population of eighty-two, I was sure the locals would know I didn't belong.

It was late when I arrived at the chained gate guided only by my headlights, which were too weak for the darkness of the night. I checked the last line on my instruction sheet: "Keep driving up the hill until you see the small church." The tiny white building with a steeple and towering cross sat on a small hill in a bed of forest and gravel. I fumbled around for the key, while muttering trembled prayers. I could not see anything, but I heard every rustle in the wind, every crunch of leaf.

Rusted chairs and old wooden podiums decorated the inside of the church. It smelled of mold. Mice scurried past my toes, and spiders the size of my fist watched me from the corners of the walls. I spent that first night staring wide-eyed at the ceiling until the sun rose, relieved when I realized I had made it through the night, although it would be another forty-eight hours before anyone would join me. It wasn't long before the rain clouds bellowed above me, and anxiety rippled through me. Without cell service, internet, or a clue of what surrounded me, I wanted nothing but to go home. In fact, I wrote it in my journal like a wish.

And then I heard it. Or maybe I felt it. Sometimes it's hard to tell the difference.

Go take a walk in the rain.

I can't tell you why, but I did.

I took a walk through the forest while rain poured down from above and the question *What are you afraid of?* pulsed inside of me like blood through veins. I named a fear with each step I took. By the time I made my way back to the church, I was filled with nothing but love for this place that had terrified me hours before—the trees, the plants, the deer and bunnies that made that place their home.

Weeks later, I started a blog documenting my trips, and I wrote that Spirit called out to me and told me to take a walk in the rain. Someone from my church read that blog, a young pastor—threatened not by my accent but by the certainty of my calling—who proceeded to write me an email questioning the idea of God speaking to me.

"But did you hear him audibly?" He questioned, followed by some things about the dangers of a new emergent church movement and a lecture about how God speaks only through Scripture. My heart sank, and my cheeks burned hot with embarrassment. I felt foolish for writing that, but something in me pushed me to keep writing the things that sounded silly to some but that were real and powerful to me.

I eventually stopped feeling embarrassed by these kinds of people, men and women alike, who wanted to extinguish the mystery of Spirit in me in order to assert their own perceptions and expectations of what they think God is like. Now I just feel pity for those who reject anything that doesn't conform to their ideas about how to know and experience the divine.

●··●··●

The story of the call of young Samuel spoke differently to me after my nights alone in the Appalachian mountains. In this story, Samuel is sleeping when he hears his name being called. Naturally, he goes to Eli the priest, who he serves in the temple, and answers him, "Here I am. What do you want?" (1 Sam. 3:5).

"I didn't call you," Eli tells him repeatedly as Samuel keeps getting up at the sound of his name. Finally, Eli realizes it is God's voice Samuel is hearing, so he tells Samuel to answer God directly: "I'm listening, LORD" he's to say (3:9). God tells Samuel that Eli's household will suffer punishment for his sons' evils. The next morning, a terrified Samuel delivers the news to Eli.

I've often heard sermons that focused primarily on Eli's mentorship of the young boy, or on where he might have gone wrong with his sons. But ultimately, these sermons praise him for his response to the news of his family's doom. A response, we're told, we ought to emulate. But I'm less interested in what I might learn about Eli than I am in gleaning the often-overlooked wisdom from young Samuel.

We're told that Samuel didn't yet know God (3:7) when he heard God's voice calling to him, but I wish I could ask him if that was really true. Did he not "know God" according to the standards that were set for him? Did he know God, just not in the way that he was expected to? There are a lot of things we say children don't *know*, but I'm learning that most of the time, that's simply our perception of what *we believe* true knowledge is.

Prior to this experience, Samuel and Eli the priest had been serving God in the temple day in and day out, engaging in the everyday-ness of their lives. But the text says, "The LORD's word was rare at that time, and visions weren't widely known" (1 Sam. 3:1). I wonder if

Samuel and Eli knew that. Or was this an observation noted in hindsight? When they lit the candles and accepted the sacrifices, did they not think God was speaking? Did they keep doing the sacred things expectant that eventually they would hear God's voice, or did they think they sensed and experienced the divine in the midst of their day-to-day rituals?

I don't imagine that Samuel—or Eli for that matter—anticipated hearing from God that night. It was dark and he was in bed and all the holy stuff had been dealt with for the day. The sacrifices had been made and the folks had come to worship and the candles had burned down to the wick. If God intended to speak, wouldn't he have done it during that time? Not in the middle of the night when the mice scurried about and the leaves rustled in the dark and things felt unsure and scary.

But perhaps that's the point. Perhaps God wanted Samuel to remain expectant. Perhaps God wanted to surprise him so that he may know that while God is certainly in the daylight, in the safe spaces, in the rituals, this doesn't mean God is not also in the darkness, in the quiet and fearful uncertainty of the night when secrets are penned into journals.

●··●··●

The groans from the baby monitor startle me awake. I nod back off after a few minutes, but the groans get louder.

I look at the time. It's 2 a.m. The alarm will ring in a few short hours and again, I'll wake up exhausted. I sigh.

A third time I hear my baby's cry from the monitor, louder than before.

"I'll go get her," my husband says, sounding equally disoriented. I lie in bed waiting for my daughter, thinking of Samuel being awakened by a voice, not expecting to hear God.

Speak, I'm listening, I pray.

I watch my daughter's eyes straining to focus on my face in the dark. She lets out a shriek of excitement when our gaze locks. She loves joining us in bed. Parenting books offer all sorts of *do's* and *don'ts* to anxious new parents: Don't bring your child into bed with you when they wake at night. Don't make eye contact with your baby so they know it's time for sleep. But tonight, I'm rejecting any advice that discourages our connection, that hinders our humanity.

I offer my daughter my breast, and our eyes stay locked until she drifts back to sleep.

I lay a soft kiss on her forehead, and hot tears sting my eyes.

Christianity offers all sorts of *do's* and *don'ts* to followers of Jesus as well; we're told not to trust visions or the voice of God outside the biblical text. As in Samuel's time, such experiences are rare, we might hear. And some may respond to talk of them with suspicion. But then the house quiets, and we're left not with the opinions of others but rather with just enough stillness to remember that sometimes Spirit calls to us in the middle of the night, in a secluded church in the forest or through a baby monitor—even and especially after all the holy stuff has seemingly been dealt with for the day.

We don't know how or when Spirit will speak, and perhaps that's the point. All that is asked of us is that we remain expectant.

- In what unexpected ways has the divine spoken to you?
- What practices might you foster to maintain a posture of listening?

Day 16

A Deeper Dimension

Can you fathom the mysteries of God?

—Job 11:7

When I was in elementary school, a teacher once told us that heaven isn't "up there" but "right here," swirling her finger in a circular motion as she signaled around the room. She said hell was here too. No, she wasn't talking about how the kingdom of God is among us, or how poor and exploited people across the globe experience a daily hell on earth (that would have been way more helpful).

She was talking about heaven and hell as real and present but in another dimension, one we cannot see. "But I think they can see us," she intoned, penetrating my nine-year-old soul. After this statement, my teacher scribbled a fraction on the board and continued with her lesson plan, unaware that my mind was spinning into chaos, the limbic area of my brain firing like fireworks on the Fourth of July.

I never saw reality the same after that, and it terrified me. Afraid that there might be an accidental glitch in the system of dimensions, I lay awake trembling night after night, worried that I might see an angel, my bisabuela (great-grandmother) Flora, or worse, *the devil*, in my bedroom as they observed us from their respective planes of existence.

I often wondered what was happening in the afterworld around me. Were there bodies burning in lakes of fire, people begging for drinks of water, while I sat on the couch unbothered, watching cartoons and sucking the milk out of soggy cookies? *What if I could find a way to cross over and offer help?* Providing assistance seemed the ultimate calling and purpose in life.

I now know that heaven and hell in other dimensions isn't an unpopular belief, but as a young kid it expanded my universe in a way I was unprepared to handle.

I knew little about the spiritual realm back then, but one thing I did know is that the things of God are far beyond what the eye can see. "Can you fathom the mysteries of God?" Job asked his friend Zophar (Job 11:7).

We cannot fathom the mysteries of God, yet throughout the centuries we've continued to speculate and build theologies and write books and somehow end up absolutely sure about what God thinks, wants, or believes.

For centuries, many Christians held the viewpoint that God's plan involved enslaving and subjugating other people. They assumed God wanted them to conquer "barbarians" and bring them into alignment with "proper" Christian practices. They were convinced that God had charged the Europeans to save the "savage" world—like it or not.

As I was educated and formed in this shadow, there was a time when I too was certain on what I believed were God's plans, God's beliefs, and what God wanted for my life—and worse yet, the lives of those around me. For too long as an adult in the evangelical world, my faith had only one dimension.

●··●··●

Because we're betting our lives on something we cannot see, our spirituality is often subject only to the mind. What can be known can be mastered, and thus, our faith becomes an intellectual endeavor. But despite how much we might try, we cannot rationalize our knowledge of God. In fact, our reasons for coming to God are less logical than they are emotional, more mysterious than they are known, intuitive rather than rational.

Most of us feel we truly know God based on the ways we've experienced God.

Flannery O'Connor once said that "mystery is a great embarrassment to the modern mind," and I've found this to be true.[1] The modern mind cannot celebrate or rejoice in mystery because it loves resolution and clarity. Perhaps this is why when I talk about God as mystery, some Christians wince, roll their eyes, and tell me that everything I need to know about God can be found in the Bible. But it's in Scripture where I most frequently encounter the mysteries of God.

Ecclesiastes tells us that God placed eternity into our hearts (3:11). What is this other than divine mystery? The truth is that mystery is innate in all of us. I don't say this simply because the Bible claims it but because we know that to wonder about what we cannot understand is a common human experience, like falling in love, like dying. So when we deny the power of mystery or the way it moves us, we deny a part of ourselves—a part created by the divine and an integral piece of the image of God in us.

"Glory to God," Paul writes to the people of Ephesus, "who is able to do far beyond all that we could ask or imagine" (Eph. 3:20). Christians believe that God is able to do more than we can imagine, yet many cling only to perceptions of God that they understand or agree with. I didn't embrace the bigness of God until I let myself be surprised by new ways of perceiving the world and the divine. However, admitting my limitations, my uncertainties, and my inability to fully know takes vulnerability. I confess this doesn't come to me naturally. As Krista Tippett writes, "Mystery lands in us as a humbling fullness of reality we cannot sum up or pin down. Such moments change us from the inside, if we let them."[2]

In chapter 19 of Exodus, God is unapproachable by all but Moses, appearing to him alone on Mount Sinai in fire and in thunder. If anyone were to even touch the mountain where God would appear, they'd die. Five chapters later, however, we encounter something entirely different: God is inviting. In fact, the text says that Moses, Aaron, and seventy elders all looked at God and ate and drank with God and were not harmed.

I've learned to love these theological juxtapositions: these multidimensional images of God that remind us of divine mystery. If I ever think I have the Spirit of God figured out, I know it means I have more listening and learning to do. The great mystery of Spirit is that there's no limit to what we can learn, know, and embrace. Steven Charleston, an Episcopal priest and citizen of the Choctaw Nation says, "There are no fences we can build around the vision of God to contain it or explain it."[3]

I mourn for those whose God is anything but mysterious. And mystery, for me, is letting go of control; it's knowing that even if I don't understand, Spirit is at work in the world. Even if I don't see, Spirit is there.

●··●··●

You know those moments when on occasion the light hits your desk at just the right angle from the window and suddenly your perspective is changed? You're awakened to a sea of a million little dust motes swirling and twinkling and altering your reality. They float effortlessly, illuminated in the sun's rays. You may not always notice them, but they never cease to be there. All it takes is some light and the right angle.

These twinkling little specks are pretty subversive if you think about it. Most of us spend our lives trying to get rid of accumulating dust piling thick on the blades of our ceiling fans. But these same particles take on a unique and curious quality when revealed by beams of sunlight. They shift our focus, beckon us into another dimension.

This is the gift of mystery and wonder.

Recognizing this different dimension doesn't need to be a lofty or complicated task. It can be as simple as catching the sun at just the right angle and at just the right moment and being awed by divinity.

- How has the mystery of God awakened or illumined your faith?
- What inspires awe in you and how might you foster that more regularly in your life?

THE BODY

Day 17

A Disabled God

❃

The body isn't one part but many.

—1 Corinthians 12:14

I remember when my daughter discovered her hands were a part of her body. She spent weeks holding them in front of her tiny face, inspecting them as she turned her wrists back and forth, narrowing her focus onto her fingers, marveling at how each one moved and twirled. She'd stare so intently her eyes would cross and her lips would purse and her brows would furrow. It was pure magic.

With time, she began to recognize that those hands were hers—a part of who she is. Those hands flailed about of their own accord only a few weeks prior, smacking her in her own face. Suddenly though, they became an invaluable part of herself—she could now grasp and explore items by sticking them in her mouth. I imagine the tiny synapses in her brain firing as she came to recognize her own body.

● · ● · · ● · ●

Bound by the ideology of empire, Western society approaches the body as something we possess. We think of ourselves as *having* a body instead of *being* one. And in this thinking festers the notion of wanting to control, conquer, and subjugate our body to fit the norms imposed on us. Our relationship to our body mirrors the way all manners of injustice and inequity play out in our society: relationships of dominance and coercion. As a result of the objectification and commodification of our bodies, we find ourselves fragmented and disconnected from who we are.

Embodiment psychologist Hillary McBride encourages us to learn to say to ourselves, "This is my body," as a first step in remembering our wholeness and affirming our bodies as the place of our being-ness.[1]

As I watch my fingers sprawling across my keyboard and look down at my feet resting on the ground, I recite those words out loud: "This is my body." I do so remembering a God who proclaimed those words while sitting around the table with his friends: "Take and eat. This is my body" (Matt. 26:26).

Our fully embodied God saw himself as his body. Communion was never separate from it.

After he was resurrected, Jesus told Thomas to touch his body, inviting Thomas to place his hands in his wounds (John 20:27).

Jesus's body was central to his existence. Salvation was never separate from it.

Terrified and doubtful, Thomas inspected Jesus's wounds. And this is the profound mystery and beauty of the resurrection: Jesus *still bears the scars inflicted on him at his death.* Jesus's *wounded* body is central to the narrative, but that body would be considered broken and deficient to dominant culture. This is the body that our faith is rooted in and the truth it reveals: broken bodies are sacred.

Theologian Nancy Eisland argues that the resurrected Jesus is revealed as the disabled God when he presents his impaired hands and feet to the disciples. This resurrected Jesus challenges the widely held assumption that once humans arrive in heaven, they will be perfect physical specimens. Heaven is not an ableist utopia. Instead, the disciples are called "to recognize in the marks of impairment their own connections with God, their own salvation. In so doing, this disabled God is also the revealer of a new humanity."[2] We are united in the breaking of bread and partaking of a sacred, broken body.

Paul says that we are one body with many parts, and it is the parts of the body we think are the weakest that are the most necessary (see 1 Cor. 12:12–27). What Paul is not saying is that there are weaker members; he is saying that those *we think* are weaker are actually the most important. Jesus's disabled body points to a new perception of others.

While we may operate as if some people are less necessary because of their perceived limitations, Paul encourages us to honor and see the value everyone brings, even and especially the ones we think of as "less honorable." It is these members of the body who are given the most honor. We do this so we may have mutual concern for one another (1 Cor. 12:23, 25).

We look after each other the way the body tends to itself. One part of the body takes care of another part of the body: our hands use a toothbrush to clean our teeth, navigate a wheelchair so we can get around, or put food in our mouths so we may eat. As with our bodies, our lives with God, neighbor, and the world cannot be understood independently of one another.

There's a story in the Bible of four nondisabled individuals who lower their disabled friend through a roof to get to Jesus (see Mark 2:1–5). I've heard sermons about how helpful these friends were or how, like them, we should be willing to do anything to get to Jesus. And perhaps those things are true. But I'm thinking about the man on the mat as more than a passive character in the story. As a disabled man, he was familiar with the barriers in place that kept him from full participation in the community, and perhaps he knew exactly how to break them. Together, the five friends found a way to overcome one of those barriers and to make a space for every body to be present with Jesus.

Like racism, sexism, heterosexism, or classism, ableism is a system of violence that stacks the deck against certain kinds of people, says Rabbi Julia Watts Belser. She explains that while ableism targets primarily people with disabilities, it haunts everyone with a body or a mind. "We are all at risk when we live in a culture that tells us we are only as good as our last success." When we talk about disability, we recognize the stake we all have in resisting a culture that asks us to be omnicompetent and "regulates the way in which we manifest and show up in our bodies—the amount of space we take up, the way we're supposed to think and feel, and the consequences for stepping out of line."[3] It is precisely a disabled God who can save us from the idols of perfection and efficiency.

I need a disabled God because my life is more than my last accomplishment, and my body is sacred and worthy outside of its ability.

●••●••●

After discovering her hands, my daughter discovered her feet and then her toes. She learned that if she flings her leg across her body with enough force, it will cause her to twist from her back onto her belly. The first time she accomplished this she looked up at me with astonishment: *Did I just do that? Was that me?* And then she smiled. I cheered.

I want to have the kind of wonder and awe for my own body that she has for hers, not just because my body is sacred but because *it is me.* I have never known an existence outside it or a reality apart from it. It is in my body that I experience the sunrise, that I feel the wind blow, that I hear the rumble of thunder, that I smell the earthiness of rain.

Part of my job as a mother is to foster my daughter's awe of her body exactly the way it is. I do so to shame a culture that says her body is no good if it isn't thin or productive or fast or strong enough.

But before I seek to do that for her, I stop to acknowledge that she has already done it for me.

- How might a disabled God change the way you value all bodies? How might it help you connect more deeply with your own body?

Getting Curious

❀

Taste and see that the LORD is good.
—Psalm 34:8 (NIV)

"Hurry, come here!"

Taylor rushes toward me.

"Do you smell it?"

We lift our nostrils; our chests balloon with breath.

It has become our morning ritual to step outside under the oak tree right as the sun rises. We inhale glory. Sometimes the smell is crisp and fragrant like the leaves of my afternoon tea, other times the smell is deep and succulent like fresh pepper straight from the grinder. But always it smells the way of earth, the way of life abundant.

I learned recently that in the modern world humans have begun to use our senses less and less as we've become more confined to the visual and the auditory—our days mostly restricted to laptops and earbuds. It's also true that we're intentionally blocking out the senses that are distasteful to us because of how many we encounter in our midst: the sound of honking horns, the sight of construction equipment, the smell of truck exhaust and factory fumes.

In more ways than one, we are disconnected from the practices of our ancestors. As ecologist Arthur Haines notes, avoiding unpleasant senses would have likely meant imminent death for those who relied on them.[1] In the past, people needed all their senses for survival, extending them as far out into their environment as they could to find both resources and protection from predators and other threats. Our needs are different today, as we experience much of the world digitally. While technology is helpful for us in many ways, it also means that we are constantly bombarded with unnatural stimuli faster than we can process them. As a preservation mechanism, we learn to shut down. This strategy applies to more areas of our lives than just our senses.

Russia is bombing Ukraine as I write this. Each morning I scroll past a new death toll before continuing on with my day. I have absolutely no idea what that is doing to my soul, but I cannot imagine it is anything good. Another disturbing figure is our losses due to COVID-19. More than six million people around the world have died as a consequence of contracting this virus. Six million.

These numbers remind me that I never want to become numb to the absurdity of death and injustice. Even if I'm not surprised by it or by the systems that perpetuate it, I don't want to simply shut down and not feel angst or be moved. I don't want to stop paying attention or live with muted awareness of my surroundings.

● ∘ ∘ ● ∘ ∘ ●

The Bible is one grand invitation to return to the ways of our ancestors. In between the stories of survival and the poems of lament are calls to engage every single one of our senses: tasting, touching, smelling, seeing, and hearing the holy. It asks us to pay attention, to live fully aware.

"Jesus reached out his hand and touched him." (Matt. 8:3)
"We smell like the aroma of Christ." (2 Cor. 2:15)
"My sheep listen to my voice." (John 10:27)
"Whoever eats this bread will live forever." (John 6:51)

My husband and I once had a celery dish that had us singing hallelujah. *Celery.* Taylor asked to speak to the chef after our meal because such creativity deserves to be recognized and celebrated. Right then and there we realized nothing is too ordinary or too bland to be outside of God's glory. *Amen.*

While we've been taught there are five primary senses, neuroscientists assert that there are upward of thirty others—some even say there are as many as fifty-three. We are sensory beings, and this

83

stretches beyond just the physical.[2] For example, we sense gravity, the passage of time, our balance, the temperature, and hunger. Like sharks or bats, some humans have even claimed to sense electrical or magnetic fields. Deeper than that, though, we can feel a sense of vulnerability, trust, belonging or the lack thereof. An extension of these that most humans can feel intuitively but cannot explain is a sense of the spiritual or the divine.

To sense this presence, we must take notice of it, recognizing when the hairs on our arms are on end or when we experience a knowing that we feel in the marrow of our bones rather than in our minds.

I'm an enthusiast for all things horror. One year, Taylor and I spent six months watching *only* scary films. It was finally Christmas before we thought it might be nice to fill our evenings with more feel-good material and less blood and guts. I looked this up—my love for horror—and it turns out there's a psychology behind it. When we consume horror, we experience stimulation. Our senses become heightened, and some of us enjoy that feeling. After several good jump scenes, I'm hyperaware of everything around me. I catch every noise and every movement.

I recognize that hypervigilance rooted in anxiety is not ideal or sustainable, but a heightened awareness grounded in the peace and wonder of knowing the sacred can be experienced in each sensation within your body. *This* is the sort of awareness in myself and in my surroundings that I want to nurture; this is the holy curiosity I am seeking to rekindle.

Curiosity is suspect in many Christian circles where people are convinced our faith rests only on following rules. It's a slippery slope, some of us have been told. When it came to my spirituality, I was taught to seek answers over and above the sacred discipline of asking questions, and this proved detrimental when I became afraid to wonder and dream about God for fear of "straying from the faith." I'm still not sure what that means. Curiosity has since become a great companion, a trusted friend who meanders along with me in kinship—in both the familiar and the unknown. We both know, Curiosity and I, that so much of God's beauty is waiting to be explored. These are the paths of discovery that take root in us and eventually become passions, callings, and vocations. In this way, curiosity sometimes even saves us, enlivening us with purpose.

"Questioning is just as vital to awareness as using all our senses," notes Haines.[3] Questions are a direct reflection of our curiosity, inviting us to keep paying attention and to live as active characters in our own story. Too many have stopped noticing the Spirit because they believe they already have the answers they need. But a holistic and robust faith is a faith that is engaged—a faith that remains curious.

● ∙ ● ∙ ∙ ●

There's a story in Exodus where God and Moses are having a conversation right after God tells Moses to leave Mount Horeb and head to a new location. Moses is frustrated by this instruction. "You've been telling me 'lead these people,' but you have not let me know whom you'll send with me," he complains (Exod. 33:12 NIV).

"My presence will go with you," God responds (33:14).

What would God's presence look like? Feel like? How would Moses be sure it was with him? I imagine he wrestled with similar questions because he proceeds to demand that God show him his glory (33:18).

And what does God show him?

His back.

Perhaps this was God's way of satisfying Moses's curiosity, but only up to a point. Being limited to seeing God's back was clearly necessary to preserve Moses's life, but I also wonder whether withholding the sum of God's glory left Moses longing for more. If he could have seen God's face and lived, would he have stopped seeking for God's presence along the way? Would he have stopped being vigilant? Maybe seeing God's back made Moses more curious about God's face, allowing him to retain his desire to know more.

Perhaps that's part of how God displays love for us. There will always be more of the sacred to know, more of the divine to be had, more glory to behold, if we just stay curious. Novelist Celeste Ng once said that curiosity allows you to "approach the world as a trove of things to take in, rather than things you frantically, fearfully wall out."[4] What sort of liberation might be found if church communities encouraged us to live this way?

In one of Mary Oliver's most famous poems, "The Summer Day," she writes, "I don't know exactly what a prayer is. I do know how to pay attention," as she sits on the grass watching a grasshopper eat sugar from her hand.[5] Perhaps paying attention *is* a form of prayer—the way to a deeper spirituality where, curious, we seek to sense God with our whole being. "Come and see what God has done," the psalmist once said (Ps. 66:5 NIV). This requires a curiosity that invites us to engage all our senses and to observe ourselves and everything around us.

"Taste and see that the LORD is good" (Ps. 34:8 NIV).

After all, curiosity is what led us to that celery dish, and we might not ever be the same.

- What do you smell, taste, hear, feel, and see on a daily basis that reminds you of the divine?
- What new discoveries has your curiosity led you to?

Day 19

Breath Prayer

❉

The LORD God formed the human from the topsoil of the fertile land and blew life's breath into his nostrils. The human came to life.

—Genesis 2:7

The land was bare, only a stream flowing through it, when the Spirit of God hovered above it. Without warning, the topsoil began to swirl like a tornado from the ground—a sight like no other. And suddenly the topsoil—black, fertile, and beautiful—began to take the shape of a human: chest and abdomen, legs and arms, fingers and toes, and then a head came into focus—eyes, a mouth, a nose. God then held this human—black, fertile, and beautiful—and in an act of deep intimacy, pressed divine lips to the human's and breathed out divine spirit, giving life to this new creation.

When God fashioned the human, there was an undeniable relationship between soil, fertile land, and breath. Meeting us in the place of dust from which we emerge and to which we return, God infuses us with this life-giving connection. Every breath we take unites us to the earth and to the divine.

●··●··●

The summer after my high school graduation, I enrolled in a couple elective courses at a community college near my house. Unsure what I wanted to study, I picked a psychology class that was titled something about being happy. It sounded perfect.

On the first day of class I sat hunched down in my desk, hoping none of the students would sense that I was fresh out of high school. Our professor glided into the room, surveying it on an inhale. He had a tangibly calming presence. We let out a collective chuckle when he told us that for our final exam we would need to master the art of juggling, and for our midterm he'd make sure that we had learned proper breathing. I relaxed my shoulders. My first thought, *This is college?* My second, *Who doesn't know how to breathe?*

The professor told us proper breathing was the greatest lesson he could teach, as not many people know how to do it correctly. I was intrigued.

Every day we'd place our hands on our bellies, release our jaws, and practice moving the air through our lungs, expanding our bellies, slowly and then quickly. We'd count our breaths and set intentions for every inhale and exhale.

I passed my midterm (and yes, I did learn how to juggle for my final exam), but something more important happened to me in that classroom. I was given the ticket to travel into myself in order to access a deeper mode of being and knowing. You see, our breath can serve as a resource of reconnection with ourselves while on a path of self-discovery, personal development, and well-being. In such a disembodied world, connecting with your breath—our very source of life—is a sacred endeavor, bringing us back into a state of embodiment and our own unique creative impulses. Breathing is deeply personal, but it is also cosmic and communal, creating coherence with others and the world around us.

To be attuned to your breath is the difference between existing and living. It mirrors the difference between aging and maturing; everyone gets older, but not everyone gets wiser. We all breathe, but not all of us are experiencing the deep, life-giving connection available to us when we do.

When we are intentional about breath work, we develop a skill that doesn't seem like a skill at all—as most people take this seemingly simple act for granted. I have been guilty of this myself, but paying attention to my breathing has been a lifeline in moments when I've needed it the most.

Why do we overlook the power of the simplest things in life?

Most Christians love stories of giants defeated by pebbles and city walls tumbling at the sound of a trumpet. We love to believe that our faith can move mountains and turn a couple pieces of bread into a feast for five thousand. We are drawn to the extraordinary and the extravagant. We want to find ourselves enveloped in the elaborate—the big moments and the big movements—because we've come to believe that these are more important. But some of the moments of deepest awareness of God and ourselves take place in the ordinary.

In meditation, we're usually instructed to focus on our breath to keep our minds from wandering. Yet isn't it profound how noticing the simple rise and fall of our bellies can cause a noticeable shift in us?

Researchers have found that our breath is *the* link between mind and body, changing every moment in response to our thoughts, feelings, and unconscious patterns. It even fluctuates when we think of past experiences that are held within our bodies. Every emotion we experience has its own distinct breathing pattern and rhythm. For example, when we are angry, our breath becomes short and quick; when we're sad, it becomes long and deep. When we're scared, we inhale. When we're pleased, we exhale.

Stress creates rapid breathing that stimulates the sympathetic nervous system, which is responsible for our fight-or-flight response. The vagus nerve is the main component of the parasympathetic nervous system, which is responsible for rest and relaxation. The vagus nerve is extraordinary, wandering through our entire body. What's fascinating to note is that information travels not from the brain to the body but up from the body—through the vagus nerve—into the brain. This means that it is our bodies that influence our minds, not the other way around. When we engage in deep breathing, we participate in our bodies' conversation by activating this miracle nerve, which in turn influences how information in our body is transported and, ultimately, how our brain and our body respond.

Our breath is the powerful and dynamic exchange between our unconscious and conscious awareness.

Breath itself is intimate; it is inside of us, with us every moment. But because we live on an oxygenated planet, our breath also joins the cycle of life that includes everything—every human, animal, and plant. Even water itself is sustained by life-breath. When we join in with our collective breath consciously and intentionally, we breathe as one with all of creation and with every other human on the planet.

The air of our common home is interconnected through atoms and subatomic particles existing among every living being in our world. Deforestation changes the level of carbon dioxide in the air, affecting the temperature and quality of the environment that sustains us. Each breath is fed to us by the earth, the earth that we are slowly choking through unsustainable and wasteful practices. When the airborne spread of COVID-19 forced us to stay indoors, high-traffic areas became less congested. Pollution and smog were at the lowest they've been in decades. COVID-19 reminded us that we all share the same air; we are connected on an intricate and intimate level.

●··●··●

One way to engage breathing as a spiritual practice is through Breath Prayer, an ancient exercise that invites us into an intimacy with ordinary tasks and habits of our day. Originally performed by ancient monastics, Breath Prayer is rooted in Paul's instruction to "pray without ceasing" (1 Thess. 5:17). The early desert monks wanted to find a way to do that, so they cultivated the practice of attaching a prayer to every single breath as a form of embodiment. "By placing a few words on the inhale and a few on the exhale, it unites the prayer with the body," writes theologian Nancy Wiens. She also notes the linguistic connection between the Spirit and our breath in Scripture, as both *ruach* and *pneuma* mean breath, wind, or spirit. "The simplicity of breathing can relieve us from complicating our prayer . . . so that we listen for God's presence and become open to it."[1]

The presence of God is not only around us but also within us. This is evident in the mere fact that God's name pronounced in Hebrew, YHWH, consists of aspirated consonants that, spoken, are like the sound of breathing. Isn't it true, then, that if Spirit dwells in us, each breath is like a prayer?

A first cry, a last word, and every single breath in between are all sacred declarations.

The beauty of praying with each breath is that it attunes us to finding God in each moment, to experiencing the divine in the simple. It turns our attention both inward and outward, to ourselves and to our interrelatedness with every being.

God is always in movement, even if we don't feel it or even—and especially—when we're not doing anything but letting our bellies rise and fall with each sacred breath.

- Inhale: My breath invites me into sacred awareness.
- Exhale: I need do nothing but breathe.

Day 20

God Moves In

❋

The Word became flesh
and made his home among us.
—John 1:14

Taylor and I packed our Kia and headed west to Los Angeles on nearly
a whim. I landed a job working with teens at a local church while
finishing my seminary studies, and Taylor was hired as a barista at a
coffee shop. We knew this wasn't enough to afford the cost of living in
our new city, but it was enough to get us out of our former situation.
We were newly married and reevaluating what it looked like to follow
Jesus when everything we thought we knew about him was unraveling.

For thirty days we slowly trekked through mountains and deserts.
We squeezed through slot canyons and did some spelunking in ancient
caves. Our marriage was tested for the first time during a sandstorm
at Lake Powell. We sat huddled in our tiny tent as it was buffeted by
gusts of wind and sand, arguing about whose idea it was to camp here.

We arrived in LA, ready to pitch our beat-up tent at the nearest
campsite when we received a phone call with a last-minute offer of a
place to stay while we figured out where we'd live. After a few weeks
with generous strangers who quickly became friends, we found hous-
ing in a small "intentional community" called Madison Square, a mile
or so from my new seminary's campus.

Living in Madison Square was a unique experience. It meant walking into your home after a long day to find tiny humans who do not
belong to you in your living room, admiring your plants. It meant
drawing shapes with chalk on sidewalks while listening to neighbors
share stories about God's provision since moving from Zambia. It
meant learning to cook for twenty-plus neighbors on the weekdays
and arguing theology over cheap wine on the weekends. It meant

knowing you could share stories, laughs, and tears at any moment by walking only a few steps from your front door.

We moved out of Madison Square after Taylor landed a new job near downtown. While excited to be in the city, we grieved the thought of not having a close connection with our neighbors. What would we do when we needed a small space heater because our old unit crashed in the dead of winter? Who would check in on the cats if we had to leave town, or water my plants as they sat lonely by the window?

What we thought we lost at Madison Square we somehow found in our new community of Node, an apartment complex full of friends who would also become a lifeline for us the remainder of our time in LA. Those years of living in close proximity taught me so much about the world. For one, being in a community wasn't always sunshine and butterflies. There were uncomfortable and frustrating times involving hard conversations, hurt feelings, and awkward silences. Sometimes folks didn't pull their load, including us. But as Shannan Martin writes, "the path toward discomfort is the path of connection." Being a neighbor is messy, but I think our well-being depends on it. At the end of the day, we want the same things: "to trust and be trusted, to be seen and believed, to be generous. We want the security that comes with knowing we aren't alone in this disorienting world."[1]

✦ ˙ ✦ ˙ ✦

The Message translation renders John 1:14 like this: "God moved into the neighborhood." I suppose "God became flesh and made his home among us," as many translations have it, is good too. But there's something poetic and powerful about God coming into our neighborhood: unpacking boxes, waving at passers by, walking our streets, and standing in line at our grocery stores. There's something special and intimate about a God meeting us on the porch with a glass of wine or tea after a long day of work.

A legal expert once asked Jesus to name the greatest commandment.

"Love the Lord your God with all your heart, with all your being, and with all your mind," he answered. In addition, "Love your neighbor as you love yourself" (Matt. 22:37, 39). The legal expert didn't ask about the second commandment, but Jesus thought it important enough to include it in his response. But this was more than just a response; it was his way of life.

You see, God didn't just tell us to love our neighbors; God put on flesh and bones and became one—inhabiting the same world we do, breathing the same air we breathe. God became fragile and vulnerable and dwelt among the ordinary. He was there in the awkward silences, when disagreements broke out, when tears fell from tired eyes.

God moved into the neighborhood.

This meant he was there for the celebrations as well: the dinner parties, the weddings, the harvesting of the food. I think this is worth noting. Some people have an image of Jesus as being serious and solemn, but I don't picture him this way. While the limited stories the Gospel writers chose to tell about him highlight only a part of who he was, we do find that he ate and drank with common folks enough that he was called "a glutton and a drunk, a friend of tax collectors and sinners" (Matt. 11:19). Jesus didn't love his neighbors at a distance; he was entangled in their messes. His life, in its richness and its depth, was prone to scandal. He didn't just piously teach lessons about how to live rightly and justly; he wrestled alongside folks about what it means to be human.

There must have been something unique about just being with Jesus, existing with him in the mundane, as we can gather from stories of the throngs that followed him around. He invited the kind of connections that we often long for—days filled with long talks about life and faith and spirituality. Moments of doing nothing other than simply being present together.

This is Emmanuel, "God with us."

It goes without saying that we live in a world in which our worth is tied to our productivity. We've been conditioned to believe that no matter what we do, it will never be enough, and this inevitably spills out into the way we live out our spirituality. We put so much pressure on ourselves to *do* like Jesus that we forget *being* like Jesus is important too. Being like Jesus requires nothing more than showing up as we are: meeting friends for dinner, taking walks through the neighborhood, and lending an ear—no talking, just listening. Being a whole human in this world, as Jesus was, requires all of it: the being and the doing.

For Jesus, putting on flesh and becoming a neighbor meant fighting for his fellow neighbors. It meant disrupting the status quo and turning over tables to defend the vulnerable, but it also meant dignifying them by feasting with them and attending their parties. As Mihee Kim-Kort writes, Jesus "with all his sads, glads, and mads . . . inspires celebration and instigates confrontation."[2] He was raw and real, and I wouldn't want the God we follow to be anything less than all of those things.

●･･●･･●

I was at a café recently where I mentioned to the server that I was hungry but not enough for an entire meal.

"Me too. Wanna split something?" the person next to me chimed in. I let out an awkward chuckle.

"Sure," I said—more a question than a response. We picked something off the menu. In that moment, I experienced that peculiar grace, the kind we can receive only in a warm meal shared with a stranger.

Stranger or not, shouldn't we always be this supportive of one another? This support, this connection, is what we mean when we talk about what being a neighbor entails.

What might a day for Jesus look like in our world? Perhaps he'd arise early to take a stroll with a friend by the lake after the fog has lifted, to notice with the others standing there the blue heron just as she's pushing off her perch with the great gust of her wings. As the heat of the day grows more intense, he might visit those in the neighborhood unable to escape the blistering sun, maybe bringing them sandwiches and water, pausing as long as they'd like for a conversation. When the morning becomes the afternoon, he might be at the school board meeting voicing his opinions about budgets and student safety. Then, as the cool evening sets in, he might drop by the local bar where the bartender has already served a few regular patrons and ask them all the familiar questions.

Maybe in the course of this day—this routine day—he would find his way into the same coffee shop where I am sitting. He'd be hungry but not enough for an entire meal. He might see a woman surveying the menu with a furrowed brow trying to decide, telling the barista she didn't want a whole meal, and he'd smile, "Me too, wanna split something?"

Day 21

Reawakening Your Wildness

✳

The two of them were naked . . . , but they weren't embarrassed.

—Genesis 2:25

I watched as my mom stood in front of the department store mirror, tears streaming down her face. I sat on the fitting-room bench, my legs swinging, barely touching the floor. Shopping for clothes with Mom often ended in tears. As she got older, her type 1 diabetes made it hard for her to keep up with the fluctuations in her body. I watched her stand in front of many mirrors and hate her naked body.

I wished to God I could make her love it the way I loved it.

I would eventually learn to feel a similar angst when I looked at my own body. I would be naked, and there would be shame.

"Who told you that you were naked?"

This is one of the first questions God directs to the first humans after they admit they hid to cover their nakedness, and it's one of my favorites. The weight of this question rests on the context; a chapter earlier, after the woman is created, the text says that they were naked and not ashamed (Gen. 2:25). This is a profound admission. We often talk about how perfect the Garden of Eden was for its lack of toil, the mutually beneficial relationship humans had with the land and animals, but I think this detail deserves more attention. Body shame is so indoctrinated in our society, could we even fathom a world without it? Could we even believe that *this* is God's *perfect* reality? I think it's worth noting, perhaps even saying out loud: *self-love was part of the original plan.* God cares about it. In fact, self-love is integral to the story.

The first revelation of shame in the human narrative is when Eve and Adam first realize they're naked. And thus, this rests at the crux of God's question. *Why is your nakedness a source of shame? Since when is your nakedness shameful?*

From Noah cursing his son's descendants because his son saw his naked body, to Jesus crucified naked as a form of humiliation, nakedness and shame are bound together from the beginning. But there is something particularly unnerving about the fact that our nakedness—our most embodied, vulnerable, intimate, and natural state—is tied to our greatest shame.

●··●··●

After his first voyage to the Americas, Christopher Columbus wrote that the Native peoples "showed no more embarrassment than animals."[1] I find this to be a very telling observation. What is it about whiteness that it wants to distance itself from wildness? After so many generations of taming, we've been completely infused with the idea that wildness is undesirable. But wildness in its truest form—naked and uninhibited freedom—is our original state of nature; it is what the first humans experienced in the garden with the Creator and the rest of the creation.

Before European colonizers arrived on Native land, people went around naked without shame. But shame was among the first lessons colonizers sought to impart, depicting bare skin as moral failure. What was once a natural way of being quickly became inappropriate, lustful, and evil. According to White colonizers, the Native and Indigenous body—the Brown or Black body—was eroticized and sexualized, seen as something that needed to be covered, "civilized," and "tamed."[2]

The truth about bodies is that there is no wrong or right way they should look. I don't imagine Adam and Eve thought much about their bodies being "good" or "bad." It is due to the constant messages we receive that we judge and shame our bodies, and the consequences are felt not just in the private sphere but also in the public and political spheres. Body-shame affects not just our own self-worth but also how we see and treat other bodies. The relationships of dominance, control, and coercion we maintain with our own bodies are mirrored in society, perpetuating the lie that some bodies are more valuable than others—privileging certain bodies while punishing others. Loving our bodies matters because only then can we accept and love the bodies of others. Only then can we truly fight for a just and equitable society.[3]

Body-shame is a learned behavior. Young children, for example, regardless of their height, weight, or shape, are not uncomfortable in their wildness, nor do they judge others on their frame. Instead, it is society that teaches them how they are to feel about nakedness, instilling in them the idea that certain shapes, sizes, and tones are undesirable. The disrobing of shame, then, is not simply an embracing of "body positivity." Instead, it involves a reawakening—a remembering of who we've always been.

●··●··●

Belonging lies at the core of shame. As Brené Brown writes, shame is "the intensely painful feeling or experience of believing that we are flawed and therefore unworthy of love and belonging."[4] This is not surprising, as belonging is what is fractured at the Fall.

Unashamed, Eve and Adam belonged to their bodies and their God before the world changed. At home in their nakedness, they communicated a deep truth to us: our bodies are our homes—the vessels where our souls reside. So what does that do to us when our own homes are the sources of our shame? How can we love ourselves and let ourselves be loved? Shame diminishes our potential for intimacy in every single aspect of life, moving us away from ourselves, each other, and the divine.

Our God was born and died naked. As a child, Jesus—naked, wild, unashamed—was unburdened by the pressures and expectations of society. At his death, Jesus's naked body was his representation of love. Those in power tried to wield his nakedness as a weapon of shame against him, but God used that shame to "both literally and intimately [move] toward humanity with strategic love."[5]

Where are you? God asked Eve and Adam when they hid their nakedness from him. When belonging was severed, God sought for them, beckoning them to come home.

Some of my earliest memories as a young child are showers with Mom. After covering our bodies with soap, she'd lift me up toward the showerhead and let my body slide off hers while we laughed and laughed under the drops of warm water. This is the original design: playful naked bodies fully at home in all of who they are. There, behind a shower curtain, we were unashamed, hidden from the disapproval of the world. After these moments there were no tears of sadness— only joy.

God's intention for us is to be free in our wildness: fully vulnerable and fully exposed, yet fully known and fully loved. This is belonging. This is self-love.

- How might you reawaken your wildness?
- What are some safe and practical ways you can disrobe shame as it relates to your nakedness?

Day 22

Eyes of Abundance

※

First take the log out of your eye, and then you'll see clearly to take the splinter out of your brother's or sister's eye.

—Matthew 7:5

For my daughter's first Christmas, we passed on an important family and cultural tradition in the giving of her first gift: a small gold pin with her name inscribed on it. Attached to the bottom of the pin is a black precious stone. Flip through any of my family's childhood photo albums, and you'll see pictures of children in diapers wearing this same piece of jewelry—sometimes on a pin and other times dangling from a gold chain, but always a black little gem attached to their bodies. They are called azabaches.

We'd already received a warning from a neighbor when I took her to Miami after she was born: "Ten cuidado, no dejes que nadie la mire sin el azabache" ("Careful, don't let anyone look at her without the azabache"). In Cuban and other Latin American cultures, this stone is believed to protect young children from the mal de ojo (evil eye). Someone with an evil eye can look at a person with envy or malice, which in turn can cause misfortune or harm to fall upon the object of their malevolent gaze.

While this may sound strange or New Age to some people within Western culture, it's one of the oldest beliefs held across different societies, including Mediterranean society. This may explain why Jesus mentions eyes so often in his teachings.

"The eye is the lamp of the body. Therefore, if your eye is healthy, your whole body will be full of light." (Matt. 6:22)

"If your right eye causes you to fall into sin, tear it out and throw it away." (Matt. 5:29)

"Why do you see the splinter that's in your brother's or sister's eye, but don't notice the log in your own eye?" (Matt. 7:3)

I find that last question especially intriguing. I've heard this text thrown around as some sort of theological jab, as if Jesus said it with a judgmental and condescending tone. We might assume Jesus had this attitude most of the time. One example is when he asks Mary after his resurrection, "Woman, why are you crying?" (John 20:15), as if he was bothered by Mary's tears. Do we assume Jesus was perpetually distant, irritated, or stoic toward people he came in contact with because this is how those who are desperate, grieving, or in need are often treated? Perhaps, instead, Jesus was acknowledging Mary's sorrow, inviting her to share with him her pain—even and especially—because it had to do with him.

The same goes for Jesus's call to notice the logs in our own eyes. What if this text was read as an invitation to inner exploration? *Pay attention to the log in your own eye. Notice that which is hindering your vision.* Isn't this a gift and an honor—to be invited by God to look within ourselves and to notice the things getting in the way of our flourishing and the flourishing of those around us?

● ‧ ● ‧ ●

In ancient Israel and during the time of Jesus, eyes were understood as metaphors for greed, envy, or judgment.[1] Thus, as Lois Tverberg notes, Jesus was probably comparing the idea of having a "good eye" with having a "bad eye," which were common Hebrew idioms.[2] To see the world with a "good eye" meant maintaining a posture of abundance and generosity—a mindset that rests in the truth that who you are and what you have is enough. To have a "bad eye," then, is to see the world through scarcity. At its core, a scarcity mentality exists within a spectrum of competition, assuming resources are finite and must be obtained at the expense of people or groups. This is the mindset of empire that insatiably seeks to gain more—more land, more control, and more power. And since there is never enough power to be had for those who desire it, the struggle for it leaves a trail of death and ruin in its wake.

The notion of scarcity was intentionally weaponized with the onset of capitalism by the dominant cultural group in order to justify unequal distribution of wealth and resources. In our modern world, a scarcity mindset plagues many of us—particularly those of us who hold marginalized identities—with the belief that we are not enough and will never acquire enough to access the opportunities available to those within the dominant culture. Scarcity is not a personal problem but a systemic one, and it's been this way from the time of the Roman Empire to today. Seeking to be liberated from a scarcity mindset requires investment in and commitment to solidarity practices across our communities.[3] Perhaps this is part of what Jesus had in mind when he invited listeners to pay attention to the log in their eyes.

In a recent conversation, a friend of mine noted that it's as if Jesus was preaching trauma-informed care, which shifts the focus from "what's wrong with you?" to "what happened to you?" *Look within. Why is your mindset one of scarcity? Why aren't you able to see that you are enough? Recognize the burdens that have been placed on you so that you may be healed.* Jesus had a holistic vision of community, which is why he created and maintained holistic perspectives like this one.

Eyes are about the heart and the soul. How we view the world affects who we are and what's going on internally. This requires we pay careful attention not only to our state of mind but to the lies that have been told to us—the ones that cause us to oppress our neighbor. It also requires that we tend to our own traumas and triggers.

This is the origin of mal de ojo.

●· ·●· ·●

I try to remember to put the azabache on my daughter when we leave the house. I certainly want to protect her from mal de ojo, but more than that, the little black stone on her chest is a reminder for me to look inward so that I might create outward change. It is a reminder to divest myself from the ways of empire that seeks to conquer and destroy, and to remember that I am enough. With this posture of abundance and generosity, I work toward solidarity in my community and the communities around me.

- What obstacles stand in the way of your achieving solidarity?
- What logs might be hindering you from engaging in individual and collective healing?

Day 23

A Question of Embodiment

❀

Is your anger a good thing?

—Jonah 4:4

It has been said that the Bible is living because it speaks to us in new ways every time we read it. I've found this to be true sometimes, but not always. Some Bible stories are so engrained in us, the lessons others have drawn so cemented in our psyches, that we skip reading them altogether, skeptical about what we could possibly learn—and with reason.

My first "shoebox project" as a kid was about Jonah. I was to cut and paste images related to the story onto a shoebox, recreating the scene as I understood it. And I surely understood it: *We aren't to disobey God or something terrible might happen to us like getting swallowed by a whale.* It's really quite traumatizing. As I get older, I become more convinced some Bible stories aren't meant for children.

But one day I decided to reread the story of Jonah with what I hoped were fresh eyes, and I stumbled instead upon yet another question from God that gripped me. This lesson was much less disturbing.

The question comes at the end of the story, but for context we might remember how it begins: with Jonah shirking God's command for him to go and speak God's word to the Ninevites. He's then swallowed and later expelled by a fish (not a whale). As a result, Jonah decides to listen to God and deliver his grand speech in an effort to get the Ninevites to change their evil ways. "Just forty more days and Nineveh will be overthrown!" (Jon. 3:4). This is all it takes for the entire city to repent: the people, the king, even the animals were decked out in sackcloth and ashes. But Jonah isn't happy about this. He's actually pretty angry. And this is why he often gets a bad rap: first for disobeying God, then for getting angry at God because everyone repented.

But a decolonized reading might remind us of the effects of colonial wounds and colonial trauma, which always have to do with the body. Nineveh was the capital of Assyria, the empire that captured Israel and forced thousands to resettle and live in exile. The Assyrians were the colonizers, if you will, known for their ruthlessness—for killing children and raping women. Apparently, their cruelty was due to their religious belief that war was an act of worship.

With this in mind, wouldn't it make sense that Jonah isn't too thrilled about preaching a message of repentance? For all he knows, those on the receiving end could—and possibly would—brutally murder him for speaking up. But it goes beyond this. God's people were familiar with the promise that God would rid them of their enemies. We read this over and over in Scripture. So as God's prophet, Jonah held on to the belief that God would surely restore peace by eliminating Israel's oppressors. That would happen not through repentance but by God showing up in power and might to defend his people and destroy their enemies.

After the city repents, Jonah admits that this is exactly why he fled to Tarshish. "I know that you are a merciful and compassionate God, very patient, full of faithful love, and willing not to destroy" (Jon. 4:2).

Bible scholar Marty Solomon points out an interesting detail about this confession. This prayer is from Exodus, and Jonah quotes it *almost* verbatim. Solomon explains that in the earlier story, after Moses chisels the stone tablets and goes up to Mount Sinai, God appears in a cloud and declares, "[I am] a God who is compassionate and merciful, very patient, full of great loyalty and faithfulness" (Exod. 34:6). But when Jonah quotes this passage, he leaves out a small part of it. Original readers and hearers would've noticed this because *surely a prophet knows his text*, especially this important part of the story—namely, the giving of the Ten Commandments.[1]

The word Jonah leaves out in his prayer is *faithfulness*, also translated from the Hebrew as *truth*. Jonah quotes God's own words back to God with the exception that God is a God of *truth*.[2] To Jonah, God is surely loving, compassionate, and gracious, but not faithful, because if God were, the enemies of Israel would be destroyed. This is where Jonah's anger comes into play: Jonah is upset because "God isn't restoring shalom to the chaos"—the chaos of evil, of injustice, of empire.[3]

Contrary to what we might have been taught, perhaps Jonah isn't just pouting because Nineveh repented. Perhaps Jonah's anger is rooted in him simply wanting to hold God accountable.

After Jonah challenges God as a God of truth, God responds.

"Is your anger a good thing?" God asks Jonah (Jon. 4:4).

Many might assume God asks this question with the same annoyed or judgmental tone as they assume God asks most questions, but I don't see it that way. For one, I don't think God is bothered by our human emotions. But more than that, God doesn't tell Jonah to stop being angry, nor does he condemn him for feeling that way.

Instead, God's question—asked with what I believe is tenderness and intentionality—is an invitation, "Is your anger a good thing?"

Maybe Jonah's anger wasn't a good thing, but this question gives us the space to wonder if maybe, just maybe, it was.

●··●··●

Years ago, when I first learned I was an Enneagram Eight, I devoured books and talks in an attempt to know more about myself. I learned how Eights—particularly female Eights—are often misunderstood as combative, aggressive, or intimidating (which, of course, we can be). But I learned that my anger, when not misplaced or out of control, often stems from the desire to see the world do right. Many of us Eights want justice and fairness. We want the underdog to win, and because the world doesn't usually operate that way, we might feel angry and just generally annoyed at how terrible humans can be.

Knowing this about myself was quite helpful. I used to experience much shame for feeling the way that I felt, especially as a woman, because the dominant culture tells us that to be "godly" we must be quiet, unopinionated, even submissive. As I began navigating my anger in constructive ways, I gave myself permission to not beat myself up but rather to investigate if (and when) my anger is a good thing or if (and when) it's not. This helped me see when my anger was destructive or hindering me from healing. In order to grow, we need to be given the freedom to investigate our emotions. I love that God does that for Jonah and, in turn, for us.

Sometimes the oppressor does repent and try to make things right—and sometimes, like Jonah, I might not think that's fair. But God gives me the opportunity to wrestle with this, to ask myself why, to get to know myself, and in doing so to get to know God better so that I may shatter any expectation of what I thought God *should* do or who God *should* be.

It allows me to see and experience God's mercy anew, even if I don't like it.

And then sometimes my anger—or our collective anger—is a good thing.

Jonah wasn't very happy about what the Assyrians had done to his people, and that kind of anger is certainly a good thing. We need to be angry at injustice because only when we feel it in our bodies can we be moved to action. Righteous anger leads to restoration and liberation.

Our healing begins—but does not end—with anger. Righteous anger begins from within; it turns over tables and calls the powerful to account.

In an interview with Krista Tippett, civil rights icon Ruby Sales says that "love is not antithetical to being outraged. . . . Love is not antithetical to anger." There are two kinds of anger, she explains: redemptive anger and nonredemptive anger. Redemptive anger moves us toward transformation and human up-building. Nonredemptive anger destroys, oppresses, and exploits. The latter is "the anger that white supremacy roots itself in."[4] And yes, any of us can get caught up in this kind of anger.

So we might wonder: Was Jonah's anger a good thing?

The story ends with God providing Jonah a shrub for shade while he is sitting outside the city contemplating his anger. God sends a worm to eat the shrub and again Jonah gets upset. God asks, "Is your anger about the shrub a good thing?" (Jon. 4: 9), and I love that Jonah is honest with God, giving us the permission to be honest with God too.

"Yes!" he says.

"You 'pitied' the shrub you didn't raise, yet I can't pity Nineveh, where there are more than one hundred twenty thousand people who can't tell their right hand from their left, and also many animals?" (Jon. 4:10–11, adapted), God asks him.

That's the end of the dialogue. We don't know what Jonah says after that. Maybe they kept their conversation going. Maybe Jonah recognized his anger had gone from good to not-so-good. Sure, the point of the story is that God is merciful, and God's mercy is a beautiful thing—and maybe even to our human minds an irritating thing—but God's mercy doesn't negate our humanity or our desire to see justice.

So I ask one last time: Was Jonah's anger a good thing? I don't think we really get an answer. What I think we get is an invitation to wrestle with God and to ask ourselves the same question: Is my anger leading to life and to liberation and to restoration, or is it leading to death?

●··●··●

This is why embodiment is so important: It is in our bodies that we feel strongly, and when we are disconnected from our bodies these emotions might feel chaotic. We might not know why we feel the things that we do. To be whole humans we must be embodied, and that includes understanding what we feel.

Part of our liberation is rejecting the colonial mindset that says that mind, body, and spirit are not connected and that our emotions don't speak the truth to us. As Hillary McBride writes, "We feel power and agency in our physicality, and we sense that we are not just observing our bodies from the outside but living through them from the inside out." This matters for our health—individually and collectively.[5]

I like to think that God's question was one of embodiment. God invites Jonah to look within himself so he can process the feelings inside of his body and try to understand what is behind them. Perhaps, then, the story of Jonah, among other things, is an invitation for us to do the same.

Day 24

God amid the Crowds

❋

A swarm of people were following Jesus, crowding in on him.

—Mark 5:24

I decided to begin seminary in my mid-twenties after a bad breakup and growing disillusionment with the religion espoused at the evangelical megachurch I was attending. Raised Catholic, evangelicalism was new to me. But it wasn't long after my transition that I began to feel growing dissatisfaction with the bright lights and shallow sermons that plagued my Sunday mornings. I was weary of church members zealous not for justice but for a place that would affirm what they already believed at the expense of others. But I still believed that if I met *just the right kind* of Christians, the ones most serious about God, the ones devoted to God's Word, and if I, too, learned *just the right way* to read the Bible and understand God, then perhaps I could experience true belonging. I naively believed seminary was the ticket to deeper communion with God and God's people.

So I packed up my Kia and drove the eight hundred or so miles to the swamps of Louisiana. I had visited New Orleans once for a bachelorette party and thought if I were to attend seminary anywhere, New Orleans would be a fun place. I knew nothing of denominations or the culture that surrounded white evangelicalism; I just knew that I loved God and that the Bible fascinated me.

During orientation week, I sat in a lecture about how to engage with the city. Ample warnings were given on how the city's "demonic presence" had a stronghold on it. To protect our walks with Christ, we must stay clear from the debauchery and the bars, where the "sinners and drunkards" hung out. *Interesting*, I thought, as these are precisely the places where Jesus spent much of his time.

New Orleans is certainly a party destination, but when it came to the demonic, the activity pointed to was limited. There was never any mention about how New Orleans was at one time the largest slave market in the United States. Positioned along the trade route of the Mississippi River, New Orleans was a hub where crowds gathered to buy and sell enslaved people. This is where children were ripped away from their parents, where young Black women were bartered by rich White men who'd take them home and rape them. This history didn't contribute to the city's demons, though. According to the Christians around me, it was the giant margaritas and Voodoo shops that did.

The oppression and subjugation of Black people are sewn into the very fabric of New Orleans, permeating everything—even the failure to prepare for and the lack of response to the devastation of Hurricane Katrina have been tied to the corruption of the local government.

Mardi Gras, one of the largest events of the Carnival celebration, is not spared from a heritage of hate and racial discrimination. In fact, one of the most famous parades of the season (the Zulu Parade) is thrown by an all-Black organization originally created because enslaved Africans were not allowed to participate in the pageants and parties.

For months following seminary orientation, I scurried in and out of classrooms, listening to lectures by White men holding ESV Bibles; I devoured books by Reformed European theologians no longer living; I stayed up until 2 a.m. writing papers with perfect Turabian citations. I did all the things I was told I needed to do to "master" theology. I followed all the rules of belonging set before me, but God felt further away than ever.

Fall turned into winter as my insides grew colder, and I became more desperate to experience something sacred—desperate for my theology to take on flesh and bones. And then something unexpected happened. Carnival season rolled around, and something awoke in me.

In the crowd of bodies, I befriended those so-called lost souls I was encouraged to avoid unless it was to tell them they needed saving. I heard the sound of God call to me from saxophones on the sidewalk and beads smacking the concrete. And it was in the midst of this chaos and celebration—in this place where the social hierarchies dividing us into separate classes was suspended—where it became clear to me that God is not confined to red-brick walls, dead theologians, and PowerPoint lectures. God was in this crowd of bodies. This subversive crowd made up of large bodies, small bodies, short bodies, queer bodies, bleeding bodies, sweating bodies, hungry bodies, abused bodies, and disabled bodies. Crowds of bodies similar to the ones that followed Jesus.

As Jesus's popularity grew, story after story tells of the crowds desperate to get a glimpse of him. And these crowds shouldn't be overlooked. As theologian Willie James Jennings says, "The crowd is everything. The crowd is us."[1]

Like most crowds, these ancient crowds were unique because they were made up of people who wouldn't normally come together: the rich and the poor, sex workers and magicians, pious folks and thieves. Living under the weight of empire, under a system that sought (and still seeks) to disconnect people from each other through hierarchy and dominance, assimilation and control, an unexpected crowd came together and something new and beautiful was accomplished. The bodies that sought to be near Jesus—religious and non-religious, young and old—all found a sense of belonging in the crowd. Jesus binds us together by moving many individual bodies into one collective body.

In no other circumstances would the crowd gather "flesh to flesh" to call Jesus's name, Jennings points out. "In Jesus and the crowd, we see the creator-creature relationship in its most naked, most powerful form—crying, screaming, creature calling to its creator and its creator giving up his own body to his creature."[2] Jesus touched bodies and bodies reached out to touch him.

Just before the crowd presses in on him in Mark, Jesus heals the demon-possessed man who lived in the tombs, a man who was known throughout the community but was banished from it. When Jesus healed the man, he restored him not just to himself but to his community as well—removing the barrier that hindered belonging. And just after the crowd presses in on him again, he does the same with Jairus's daughter, who is ill and dying. All are restored to community and belonging.

What I had been looking for in the classroom I found in the crowd, in the midst of sweaty, inebriated bodies. God met me where warm breath stirred cold air and beer spilled onto the pavement, outside of the confines of the barbed-wired fence where we met for class lectures and chapel services.

I continue to find God in a motley collection of people drawn to intimacy with Jesus. I have a place in this crowd. It is among them where I find that my desire for Jesus also means I desire the best for the distinctive, diverse, and beautiful bodies around me.

- What unexpected crowds have stirred belonging in you? What did this speak to you about the sacredness of bodies?

WISDOM

Day 25

The *Genius Loci*

After Jacob got up early in the morning, he took the stone that he had put near his head, set it up as a sacred pillar, and poured oil on the top of it.

—Genesis 28:18

The air, the smell, the trees, the drawn-out syllables of the locals: all of it was unfamiliar. The paint was still fresh in our new house, and the walls were still bare. It felt even emptier since losing our cat, Scully. My days were lonely, spent desperately trying to make it feel like home: rummaging through boxes, walking the neighborhood, googling local meet-ups.

On one of these days, during our neighborhood walk, my husband and I met a precious elderly couple and their aging dog, which they carried in their arms because he was too old to walk on his own. We chatted about the community, our pets, and my growing belly. After some time, we said our goodbyes and continued in opposite directions.

Nearing the end of our route, reflecting on the delightful encounter and how badly we needed it, we wondered if we'd ever run into our new friends again. And then there they were, huddled around a small crowd that was congregating by our fence. "Have you met your neighbors yet?" they asked. We hadn't until this moment. The sun set behind us as we chatted, exchanged numbers, and planned puppy play dates. The elderly couple watched us all—neighbors becoming friends—with a look of satisfaction. As they walked away, I called out to them, "Hey, where do you live?"

"Oh, we're just down the way," the old man said smiling, as they disappeared over the hill.

Taylor and I got into bed that night feeling content and hopeful. It was the first time our house began to feel like a home.

"Do you think they were angels?" Taylor asked.

114

We laughed.

"Maybe," I said.

That was two years ago. We've hoped to chance upon the couple again while walking our daily route, to tell them something more than thank you. But we haven't seen them since, and maybe that's the way of angels.

●●●●●●

In Genesis 28, Jacob falls asleep on a rock and has a vivid dream about angels. In the dream, God promises him that his descendants will be as numerous as the dust of the earth and will spread out in all four directions—blessings that speak to a life of longevity and provision. On waking, Jacob recognizes the dream was sacred and utters a phrase that has become my refrain: "The LORD is definitely in this place, but I did not know it" (v. 16).

I'm drawn to the Bible's stories because they reflect the nuances and complexities of the human experience. Even the so-called patriarchs, canonized for their notable faith, had relatable moments. Characters in Scripture experienced every emotion we do. Their mistakes mirror ours as well. And despite the direct access it seemed most of them had to God, they are even still found oblivious to divine presence. This is comforting, albeit frustrating.

I often wonder how many sacred places I've been in but didn't recognize them as such because, well, because I'm human. Because I was distracted, busy, or simply because I didn't anticipate God's presence. Perhaps this isn't entirely my fault. Many of us have been taught that God is present only when God is explicitly named or when something is explicitly "Christian" (in the narrowest sense of that word), as if Jesus were like a spirit you must summon. But the reality is that divinity is all around us and within us. Sacred spaces are simply the meeting places where we enter into conversation with the divine.

After Jacob makes this realization, he thinks to himself, "This sacred place is awesome. It's none other than God's house and the entrance to heaven" (Gen. 28:17). He then grabs the rock he used as a pillow and makes an altar of remembrance. After consecrating it with oil, it becomes a sacred pillar. This, too—creating altars of remembrance—has become a grounding practice for me.

Throughout history, altars have served as the "sacred center" for people's lives—feeding, nourishing, and sustaining their spirits. At the heart of these altars lies the relationship between the physical and the spiritual. Wherever they are located, altars bless spaces and announce "a spiritual presence overseeing the activities at hand." Once created and established, they become "active sites of healing energy."[1] Part of this is the process of intentionality, of being an active participant of blessing and consecrating, of naming the space as sacred. This is part of what gives it its power, where the spirit of that place continues to live on.

It's a widely held ancient belief that alongside people, places have spirits. As David Whyte describes it, the spirit of a place "is the conversation of elements that makes a place incarnate, fully itself."[2] This is the ancient definition of "genius."

In our modern world, we've often heard "genius" used to describe individual people with high IQs, but in the ancient world it referenced the spirit of a place—its *genius loci*. This describes more than just physical geography, it includes the intangible quality of a place, it's particular ambiance. It refers to every single element converging together to create holy ground: the way the sun shines and the breeze hits your skin along with the smell of the earth beneath you. The *genius loci* of a place is unique because it exists nowhere else on the planet but in that sacred place.[3]

The morning after my encounter with the angel-neighbors, I gathered six small stones from the place where we met and built a tiny altar in remembrance. *This sacred place is awesome*, I thought. *An entrance to heaven.*

Grief and loneliness would linger in our lives a little longer as we'd lose more loved ones within a matter of months—far from any community that could offer comfort. But every time I stepped outside and saw the tiny altar still nestled by the fence, I remembered that any moment or any place can become holy ground. That flicker of hope would ignite, and the *genius loci* of that holy place would come alive: the cool of the evening, the warmth of new friendships, the yaps of happy pups—the night it first felt like home.

●··●··●

One of the local meet-ups I found during my Google searches those first few weeks was a prenatal yoga group that met a few blocks from my house. I was desperate to find a community to welcome my child into, so I began attending religiously. Each week, the eight or so of us pregnant people, most of us new to the experience, came together to lay out our fears, whisper our doubts, and proclaim our truths. We talked about losses we were grieving, the traumas some of us experienced through infertility, and the process of healing "mother" wounds. Every time we folded over into child's pose or laid back for final Savasana, tears would slide warm down my cheeks. I knew I was on holy ground. That small, dimly lit room became a sacred space where strangers became friends.

If the *genius loci* is the merging of every detail that makes a place fully itself, then human genius, too, lies at the intersection where all the elements of our life join together. It includes every moment and every experience that has shaped and formed us: our ancestors, our landscape, our language, our grief, our joys, our stories. Our *genius* is the totality of our experiences—all of it mingling and converging, existing nowhere else on the planet but within us—the meeting place where we enter into conversation with the world.[4]

The night Jacob dreamed about angels wouldn't be the only time he encountered the sacred. In fact, not too long after this, Jacob would wrestle with the divine and it would change everything for him: from his own name to how he related to God. But the difference, this time, is that he knew it. After that life-changing encounter, Jacob would consecrate that place, too, naming it Peniel because he "saw God face-to-face and his life was saved" (Gen. 32:30). This is the wisdom of sacred spaces; they are places of remembrance that shape us into who we become. When we enter into that divine conversation, we are forever changed.

This is what happened in that yoga room. The healing we experienced was not just our own but for the lives developing inside of us, the lives that now call us *mama*.

God was there, and this time, like Jacob, I knew it.

- Where have you encountered sacred spaces? How has it brought about healing in your life?
- Are there any spaces meaningful to you where you can construct your own altar of remembrance?

Day 26

Eternal Life

Everyone who lives and believes in me will never die. Do
you believe this?

—John 11:26

My abuelo (grandfather) died when my mom was in her teens. In an
attempt to spare her the pain of seeing him dead, some family members
physically held her back at his funeral, but she screamed and hollered
and squeezed her thin, flailing arms through the holes of her jacket in
order to escape from their grip. When she made it to the casket, she
beat it like a resurrection drum with every ounce of her being.

"¡Papi! ¡Papi! ¡Papi!" she pleaded as four men pried her off.

The morning after her father died was Christmas. In a fit of rage,
Mom tore apart the tree, ripping its limbs and sending ornaments
exploding onto the tile like grenades. Some would say this was inappropriate, but what truer, more human response is there to the
heartbreak of loss—especially when others have tried to shield you
from the pain of it?

●··●··●

I was a kid when my bisabuela (great-grandmother) Flora died,
and even though I lived with her, I wasn't invited to attend her funeral.
Instead, I sat home alone wishing to God I could say my last goodbye.
I hated that I couldn't. I refused to cry the days and months after her
death because I did not want my family to know how much my grief
affected me. And no one questioned this, despite the relationship I
had with her.

On most days after school, Abuela Flora and I spent our afternoons
playing hide-and-seek. Her short, elderly, plump frame hid from me

behind the door while I'd pretend not to see her or hear her breathing. After several "¿Donde estas?" (Where are you?) she'd peek her face through the crack. We'd laugh and laugh before laying on her recliner so she could give me cosquillas (tickles).

My memories of Abuela Flora were filled with warmth and joy, but only when I became an adult did I learn the whole story. You see, Abuela Flora died from old age but not before making several failed suicide attempts. The trauma of exile, of leaving everyone and everything she knew behind in Cuba during a time of economic and political unrest, was enough to set her mind on fire.

Our stories hold deep beauty. Our stories also hold deep pain.

Death carries a particular trauma, wounds and scars that feel too deep to tend to. This is why I was taught to avoid it, to move on as quickly as possible from the discomfort it brings. Life is seemingly bearable this way.

While this is an area in need of healing in my family, I know we are not alone. In the West, death is treated as a defeat, a failure of some kind. We distance ourselves from the dead and dying like a plague, stripping them of their power, minimizing the dignity and value of their lives.

We offer platitudes and assurance of resurrection to those who are grieving, but these fail to offer space to acknowledge pain and honor the lives of those now gone. And while the notion of resurrection connotes hope, it should never eclipse the sacredness of death. After all, it's a necessary precursor.

In most ancient cultures, death is understood as the holy passing from one spiritual realm to another. In the biblical world the dead were spoken of as "going to sleep"—where they would simply wake up in another realm. Burial practices suggested that even after death, maintaining contact with the community was of utmost importance. This is why one must be buried in their native land, and more importantly, with their ancestors.

Jacob gives detailed instructions about this: "I am soon to join my people. Bury me with my ancestors in the cave that's in the field of Ephron the Hittite," he tells his sons in the moments before he dies, knowing the exact history of the spot he has chosen (Gen. 49:29). These were his "last words" before taking his final breath. We might think this odd, but it is deeply telling of a people tethered to a community past and present.

To be buried with one's family and rest with one's ancestors was considered a great honor (e.g., 2 Kings 14:16; 2 Chron. 21:1). As Rabbi Danielle Upbin notes, "All of Jewish understanding was first forged through their ancestors' direct experience of God."[1] Hebrews 11 confirms that faith in God is deeply connected to the faith of those who came before us. "Faith is the reality of what we hope for, the proof of what we don't see," it says in the first verse, serving as a reminder that faith is risky. As Rachel Held Evans wrote, "At its best, faith teaches us to live *without* certainty and to hope *without* guarantee."[2] But the biblical text continues: "The elders in the past were approved because they showed faith" (Heb. 11:2). While faith might be risky, the lived experiences of our ancestors are our guides, showing us that sometimes that risk is worth taking.

As a people that belongs to God, we are continuously called on to remember what our ancestors have been through and the wisdom they impart. This is why rituals that honor our past hold so much weight: they are portals into deeper knowing; they help us tell our stories.

Setting aside the idea of death as defeat is central to living fully.

Ancestral wisdom is often passed down through oral tradition. Prescribed by the customs of a community, rituals ground us and give shape to our identity as a people. They provide order to our beliefs.

Like the Israelites, many Indigenous communities engage in rituals during major life events like birth and death. One of the most widely known is Día de los Muertos, which honors the dead with festivals and lively celebrations that draw from both Indigenous Aztec and Catholic traditions. The dead belong to the community and wake from their sleep in the afterlife to celebrate alongside their loved ones. Through these celebrations, Día de los Muertos acknowledges that death is part of the natural cycle of life. It reminds us that we are tethered to a community of people who help us make meaning of our own existence.

Chicana activist Yreina Cervántez explains that in ancient Mesoamerican lore the human spirit at the time of death transformed into a winged creature like a butterfly or hummingbird—the person's energy returning to the universe as a form of reciprocity.[3] In the same way, ancestral wisdom passed on after death speaks to this reciprocity. It acknowledges that life on earth continues to reverberate like an echo even after death.

In her podcast *Café with Comadres*, my friend and fellow theologian Karen González reminds listeners of the first law of thermodynamics, which says that no energy in the universe is created or destroyed. According to physicist Aaron Freeman, this means that after we die, "all of our energy, our vibrations, every bit of heat, every wave of every particle . . . remains in this world."[4] González builds from this: "All of that energy that our ancestors gave off as heat is still here. It's still part of all that we are. Our ancestors are with us."[5] Not only are they with us spiritually, but science confirms that they're still physically with us too—just in a different form.

God is the author of all things, even the first law of thermodynamics. I like to think, then, this is part of what Jesus meant when he said we "never die." Of course, this entails resurrection, but perhaps Jesus also meant that our energy, our heat, and our vibrations continue to remain present in the world even after we're gone. Maybe this is a part of what "eternal life" is all about.

● ● ● ● ● ● ●

I honor the complexity of life and the sacredness of death as I recline with my daughter, offering her cosquillas. I keep pictures of Abuela Flora in her room and tell the stories of her ancestors: of exile, of afternoons spent playing hide-and-seek, fully embracing the joy of life in the midst of the sorrow. I look forward to the day my elderly body can hide behind doors, my breath giving me away to my great-grandchildren—if I am so blessed with the longevity to experience this.

We honor the living by remembering the dead: the risky faith that sustained them and the stories and lessons they've passed on to us and that we continue to pass on.

We are both ancestors and future generations.

Our Celestial Siblings

[The magi] asked, "Where is the newborn king of the Jews? We've seen his star in the east, and we've come to honor him."

—Matthew 2:1–2

Stars glitter in the sky like a million little winks. The heavens are full of secrets that we desperately wish to know: *Is there anyone else out there? How does it all hold together?* Our planet is but one in a vast ocean of celestial bodies, and stopping to think about that might make you dizzy with wonder.

I remember the first time I escaped the glare of city-light pollution and was introduced to the symphony of stars with my naked eye. It was like wiping the dark smudge from my eyeglasses, my vision unhindered for the first time. Before then, stars existed only in books and in my imagination. My little sister had a fascination with space, so she taught me all about them during trips to and from the planetarium. Thanks to her, I could identify the Big Dipper, the Little Dipper, and Orion's Belt on a paper star map, but something shifted in me when I saw them right there, right above me. We were on a family beach trip a couple hours from home. With my back nestled into the sand, the sound of waves in my ears, and awe in my eyes, I was changed.

You may have heard it said that we are stardust. I used to think that was just a lyric from a song, a poetic phrase for a coffee mug, but then I learned that it's true: we are actually made of stars. Those that go supernova are responsible for creating many of the elements of the periodic table, including those that make up the human body. Put another way, nearly all the elements inside us were formed in a star, blasting through space and into our bodies once those stars died.

Maybe that's why something in us resonates with them, why we can't help stopping to marvel when we look up on a dark night. We are made of the same things.

Our universe contains billions of galaxies with billions of stars within them that are millions of light-years apart. Because they are so far away, it takes years for a star's light to reach us. When you look at one, you're actually seeing what it looked like years ago. It's possible that some of the stars you see tonight don't even exist anymore, and the ones you do see are likely bigger and brighter than the sun. If ever I want to be humbled, I remember these facts and remain ever amazed.

It's no wonder humans across time have attached meaning to our celestial siblings. Many communities and cultures have gods connected to the stars and entire religions formulated around them. Astrology played an integral role in ancient culture, including that of Jews and Christians who reckoned with the meaning of celestial events, offering elaborate theologies to make sense of them.[1] In late antiquity, Jewish sages acted as court astrologers and synagogues often featured zodiac images, some even placing these star charts in prominent positions.[2]

Christians today might marvel at the stars but scoff at the idea that they could offer us any divine wisdom. But the Bible shows us that the devout are regularly instructed to look to the heavens for information. In Luke 21:25, Jesus says, "There will be signs in the sun, moon, and stars." Celestial bodies often act as a sacred script in the sky, written for the faithful to read.

In Genesis, for example, stars are a sign for Abraham and Sarah that they will indeed bear numerous children and that the world will be blessed through them.[3] In Daniel, astrology is given to the prophet as a mode of knowledge, a path of "wisdom and understanding" (Dan. 1:20). While astrology might seem like a pagan practice to many Westerners, biblical scholars note it was not among the forbidden "occult arts" in the Hebrew Scriptures.[4]

A story about stars that has always gripped me is that of los tres reyes magos (the three wise men or magi) in the narrative of the birth of Jesus. Nativity scenes often show a small crowd of people pleasantly circling the baby and his parents. While shepherds, animals, and angels might make sense, there's something strange about the fact that astrologers are present.

We know these "wise men" came from the east, presumably the region of Babylon, where astrology was thought to have originated. Thus, they would have been drawn to Judea not just by a bright star in the sky, but by a sign with astrological significance, particularly because a new astrological age was on the horizon. Most people during this time would have been familiar with this impending change as it was common knowledge in that culture. The star of Jesus, then, must be understood within the context of the casting of regal horoscopes.[5]

Astronomers and historians have pointed out that around this exact time in history, an eclipse of Jupiter by the moon in the constellation Aries began entering Pisces—and this, some have suggested, might have been what the magi followed. This nod to Pisces is an interesting one if you think of it in the context of Jesus. For one, Pisces is a water sign, and its symbol is the fish. Jesus is known as the Fisher of Men, and his early followers used the fish as a secret symbol to identify themselves. In traditional horoscopes, Pisces is the final sign and encompasses all the others. Because it is understood as a culmination of the zodiac, people born under this sign are characterized by empathy, compassion, sacrifice, and service to others. It is the sign that represents faith and spirituality. These characteristics and values were believed to be strong during the Piscean Age—the time when Christianity dawned and during which it flourished.

Maybe all these connections are merely coincidence; maybe they're not. What's important is having the faith to believe in a God so far beyond our ability to fathom that even the stars speak to us something sacred—including the ones whose twinkle we still marvel at even though they may be long gone. God is so far greater than our ability to comprehend that even astrologers are called to be present at the incarnation. Such a God should make us appreciate wonder, be amazed with mystery, and soak in the grandeur of divinity.

The story of los tres reyes magos might communicate these great truths to us, reminding us that if we believe in a God of infinite wisdom, then why wouldn't God's wisdom be found in the stars— through science, in horoscopes, or when we look up on a dark night?

These ancient astrologers not only sought celestial wisdom to get to Jesus, they also enacted their own by disobeying Herod. To spare the baby's life, they returned to their country by another route in order to avoid having to tell the king where Jesus was. Civil disobedience against oppressive leaders is a common theme in the Bible, just ask the midwives who acted in defiance of the Egyptian pharaoh's orders in Exodus.

The presence of the "wise men" at Jesus's birth proclaims the reality that no one is outside the bounds of belonging, not pagans or astrologers or any other person or group we might have tried to cast aside. This is the depth of the incarnation of Emmanuel, who is "God with us."

●•●••●

The obvious truth is that the divine invites and calls and leads us on sacred journeys in beautiful and mysterious ways. Embracing this can expand our view not only of who God includes but also of what forms of wisdom God uses to speak and move among us.

Chet Raymo writes, "This night, like every night, is a revelation for those with eyes to see. No heavenly choir can possibly add to the grandeur of the universe itself."[6] Like the magi, we watch the night sky with wonder and awe at the miracle of divinity represented by the multitude of stars, our celestial siblings.

- In what ways has ancient wisdom surprised you? In what ways has it ministered to you?

Day 28

The Cycle of Time

Don't let it escape your notice, dear friends, that with the Lord a single day is like a thousand years and a thousand years are like a single day.

—2 Peter 3:8

When I was a child, boredom weighed on me like a burden. For hours, I'd stare at the glow-in-the-dark stickers on my ceiling, creating entire worlds in my imagination. Summer days often felt long at Abuela's house, where I would read books for hours on end and listen to the music blast from my boom box, waiting for my favorite song to play. Time felt endless.

We soon depart from long afternoons of building with Legos and blowing bubbles and find ourselves in the assembly line of adulthood. Not all of us are lucky enough to have this kind of free time, though. Whiteness worships excellence, and even some of my young friends were burdened by a striving for perfection—shuffling from one extracurricular activity to the next, only to plop into bed on weeknights as exhausted as their parents, robbed of the carefree days of childhood. I admit that in my ignorance I envied my friends with all that money—the ones who danced ballet, played softball, practiced the piano, and still managed to complete all their homework every night after school.

I didn't know it back then, but that boredom of mine was something sacred. The gift of time was invaluable.

• • • • • •

Colonial capitalism put a price tag on bodies and fenced in the land—convincing us it could be owned and calling it "private prop-

126

erty." The natural world became a resource for consumption. Here today, gone tomorrow.

In the modern Western world, time is seen as linear and fixed, moving in one direction without repetition: past, present, and future. Time is here and then it is gone, never to return again. The origins of linear time as we know it have been traced to empire, created by those looking to maximize investments and returns in their travels around the globe. We've learned to hurry because even our time is money, and so we rush all the way to our graves. But I don't want to die in a hurry.

Many civilizations, however, have understood time—both cosmic and human—not linearly, but as rhythmic, revolving around cycles such as seasons. Just look at our most common time measurement systems: the repetition of seconds to minutes and minutes to hours and hours to days and days to weeks and weeks to months and months to seasons and seasons to years.

Since the dawn of creation, humans have measured time by observing the natural world. The day and night cycles have regulated our lives. Along with our hormones, they tell us when it is time to sleep and when we should be productive. While these patterns are still present in our modern culture, they've become part of the larger structure of linear time, still fixed and static, still here and then gone. But what if we understood time the way our ancestors did? Like the tide that disappears and then appears again. A pattern that always repeats itself. All things that were will eventually be again.

The author of Ecclesiastes states this insight succinctly:

> Whatever has happened—that's what will happen again;
> whatever has occurred—that's what will occur again.
> There's nothing new under the sun. (Eccles. 1:9)

One of our Creator's very first miracles was to paint a spectacle of orange, pink, blue, and yellow across the sky in a cacophony of splendor: separating light from dark to create sunsets and sunrises.

I don't take these lightly. It is to our benefit to savor the moments we catch the sun ascending or retreating over the horizon, soaking in the glory of it all. Technicolored skies have inspired everything from award-winning nature photos to proposals to Easter morning gatherings. I often think of what a grace it is that we get to experience this miracle *every single day.* However tumultuous life can feel, we receive the gift of knowing that dawn will break tomorrow, the day after that, and then again the day after that. Isn't it like the divine that this would be so? And isn't it like us in the rush of everyday life that this miracle would become so ordinary, so overlooked, so taken for granted? I want to "unlearn hurrying"—as Robin Wall Kimmerer says—in such a way that I learn to marvel at the slow miracle of a sunrise every time it happens, every single morning.[1]

Have you ever noticed that when God separates the light from dark on that first day of creation it's the evening—the sunset—that always comes first? It's a small detail in the Genesis creation story, but it isn't insignificant. Time as we know it is turned on its head: *the day begins at night.*

While this concept may be new to Christians, Jewish tradition knows it well: every week, Sabbath begins in the evening. Reorienting our days this way serves as a sacred reminder that our day isn't to start when we open our eyes but when we go to bed. *Our days are to begin with rest.* In a culture where not even a minute must go to waste, we learn from the creation story that our value and worth doesn't come from what we produce but who we are. This is what "rest" is all about: trusting in the goodness of creation and that it will take care of us.[2]

And this extends beyond humans to the land and the animals as well. In the Bible, God commands that both are to preserve the Sabbath. Land and animals aren't to be exploited but upheld with dignity—a far cry from what we experience today. In God's economy, people aren't to take what they want and then move on; rather, they must treat the natural world with fairness, respecting its cycles of rest and its cycles of work. This holistic approach ensures longevity. The essential idea presented in the Bible is that each generation is required to maintain the world around them in such a way that it is as healthy and beneficial when they pass it onto the next generation as it was when they received it.

●・・●・・●

I caught the sunrise this morning in an effort to remember these truths: The sun will set and then it will rise and then set again. The seasons will come and they will go and they will come back again. The moon will wax and wane and the tides push and pull again and then again. Surrendering to this flow loosens the colonizers' grip from my neck, reminding me of the inherent goodness of creation. It shifts my focus from how much I might produce for myself toward how I can contribute to the whole—the overall health and well-being of our future.

We are both ancestors and future generations.

- Have you ever looked to honor the cycle of seasons and time in your life?
- What might surrendering to this pattern and this flow look like?

Day 29

Rooted in Place

> The human named all the livestock, all the birds in the sky, and all the wild animals.
>
> —Genesis 2:20

I was captivated the first time I met the wild exotic birds while standing outside my small bungalow in Southern California. *Are those parrots?* I couldn't believe it. I stared, mouth ajar, at the bright-green colony of winged creatures, flocking in the trees above my head with a fervor that left a mark on my soul.

How in the world did this many parrots end up colonizing the outskirts of downtown Los Angeles? At the beginning and end of each day, with clocklike regularity, they perch overhead squawking so loud they make windows rattle.

Legend has it a few red-crowned parrots escaped a burning aviary in Pasadena in the sixties. They haven't left, multiplying by the thousands instead. Most people in the area find the sight of them incredible at first, stepping outside to gape at the spectacle in the sky. But soon—very soon—the squawking starts to clatter in your ears too early in the mornings and too late in the evenings, and you find yourself imagining a way to eliminate these critters you once found so captivating. I'm embarrassed to admit I felt that way too, especially on mornings when coveted sleep was interrupted by unwanted trills and whistles.

And I don't think humans are the only ones who feel this way. Every once in a while, I'd find a parrot lying dead on the lawn surrounded by a gang of crows, as if to remind the parrots who's boss, whose streets and trees they're encroaching on. Originally from northern Mexico, these wild birds have made this place their home. Now rooted in a land once foreign, they've earned both their right to stay and their rightful name: the Pasadena Parrots.

There's a story in my family about the last name Armas. Apparently, it was originally the more common surname De Armas. The story goes that the "de" was dropped accidentally when my ancestors immigrated. Government officials neglected to include the particle at the beginning of our name on the documents, changing our name forever.

I didn't learn this story until recently, but perhaps I carried this knowledge in my body, as I didn't want to lose another piece of my identity. When I got married, I didn't change my last name to my husband's. My father was not present at my birth or during my childhood, so the name Armas is my mother's name. As a woman with her mother's maiden name, my attachment to the name Armas meant too much to me to let go of it.

My last name holds stories of place. It carries with it a legacy of movement, of migration. It tells the story of a single mom raising her daughter with the help of her community, among people who were also exiled and were attempting to set down new roots. It tells stories of survival.

In Jeremiah 29, God sends a message to the people living in exile: "Build houses and settle down; cultivate gardens and eat what they produce. . . . Promote the shalom of the city where I have sent you . . . because your future depends on it" (vv. 5, 7, adapted). Jeremiah encourages the exiles to establish themselves in their non-native land, which includes working to build a new life together. "They needed to stop living out of their suitcases, begin establishing roots, affirm, maintain and continue ties of family," writes theologian Monica Jyotsna Melanchthon. Most importantly, they needed to "work towards peace and community building in their own neighborhoods."[1]

In most versions of the Bible, the word *shalom* is often translated as welfare or peace, but the Hebrew concept of *shalom* implies a sense of wholeness, it communicates a relationship of completeness in both spirit and materiality. It is inner and outer peace and well-being. To seek shalom is to tend and cultivate. In exile, it involved seeking the wisdom of place: knowing the names of plants and animals and ancestors indigenous to the land and being familiar with its past and tending toward cultivating hope for its future.

● ● ● ● ● ●

"What's the name of that tree?" I asked Taylor, pointing to the burst of ivory decorating the sky. It sat among a canvas of brown and gray branches stretching across the clouds—the arms of dead oaks waiting for their turn to bloom.

"Oh, that's dogwood," he told me, telling me that they are indigenous to the region where we now live. We didn't have these in the tropical landscape where I grew up. *Dogwood*. I whisper her name every time I pass her by. I hold her name close.

I used to be really bad at remembering names—of places and people. I'd explain this when I met someone just in case I'd have to remeet them soon after. But over the years, remembering names has become a spiritual practice for me, because to remember someone's name is to honor their identity—their personhood. But more than that, to remember a person's name is to honor the community they come from and their ancestors. I now pay close attention when someone tells me their name because to name is to notice, to have regard. As Maria Popova writes, "To name is to love."[2] When we name a thing, we "confer upon it the dignity of autonomy while at the same time affirming its belonging with the rest of the namable world; to transform its strangeness into familiarity, which is the root of empathy."[3]

In many creation stories, including the Christian one, naming was the first task given to humans by our Creator. It is a sacred act and the first way of knowing, "a mode of sacramental communion with the world."[4] God not only knows us humans by name but also every beetle and weed, every tree and every mammal. And God is also named. While in the desert, a marginalized and mistreated Hagar is met and cared for by God. As a response, she gives God the name *El Roi* (the God who sees). Naming is intimate and necessary to being in community—but it's only the first step. The crucial first step in the process of knowing.

I currently sit on the traditional land of the Tsalaguwetiyi, the eastern band of the Cherokee people who knew more than just the names of the land and the animals that were a part of their kin. Like them, I want to know about all that is alive around me. This is how I root myself in place. To become one with this land, I must seek its *shalom*. I must know who struggled here, who took care of her before me. This is what it means to be fully present—to know the stories of resistance that flow from the streams of which I drink and the soil from which I eat. I do this to better serve her future.

Robin Wall Kimmerer imagines how Native elders might have viewed European colonizers arriving on their homeland: "The problem with these new people is that they don't have both feet on the shore. One is still on the boat. They don't seem to know whether they're staying or not." We must set aside these colonial ways and become indigenous to place, she argues. Can we "learn to live as if we were staying? With both feet on the shore?"[5]

● ● ● ● ● ● ●

My neighbor Jessie is an older Black woman well known in the neighborhood where we live. I met her the first week I moved in.

"Hello little lady! How far along are you?" she called out to me one day from her second-floor balcony across the street. We became instant friends, sharing Diet Cokes and stories on hot summer days about how much the city has changed. "When I moved back after my daddy died, I barely recognized this place, but I haven't left again since," she once told me. "These are my streets." I thanked her for welcoming me into her neighborhood. I meant it.

"Oh, she is beautiful! What is her name?" Jessie asked a few days after my daughter was born. I told her.

"Oh, that's my brother's name! Well, it's his street name," she whispered, smiling. "Now, I'll never forget it."

What a gift, I thought.

Every morning, as we step outside to welcome the day, I hear my daughter's name sung from Jessie's lips. Proclaimed like a promise from across the street. Every single time I hear it, I know I'm home.

- Whether you are native to the land you live on or not, how might you familiarize yourself with its past and tend and cultivate it for the future?
- How might you work toward peace and community building in your neighborhood?

Day 30

A New Moon

Blow the horn on the new moon,
    at the full moon, for our day of celebration!
Because this is the law for Israel;
    this is a rule of Jacob's God.

—Psalm 81:3–4

I lie still as a board on the table while the acupuncturist pierces my skin with needles. I don't look down once during the entire hour they poke out of me like porcupine quills. I try to focus solely on the controlled rise and fall of my chest so as to prevent my mind from spiraling and my body from dashing out the door in a moment of weakness with needles still dangling from my skin.

Despite my aversion to needles, I decided to try a session of acupuncture out of pure desperation. I was full-term in my pregnancy and had been experiencing debilitating back pain since the first trimester. By the time I reached my due date, I could barely walk, get out of bed, or turn over in my sleep. I was willing to try anything.

"When are you due?" she asked as she pulled a needle out of my skin.

"Any minute now," I answered, exasperated.

"Well, tomorrow's a new moon," she said, dabbing a tissue on the tiny wound where a speck of blood had pooled.

"Is it?" I winced.

"Yep. Babies love to be born on new moons." She smiled. It was Tuesday.

I went into labor on Wednesday.

● ● ● ● ● ●

For decades, Christians have been waging culture wars on everything from Harry Potter to the Enneagram, warning us that the devil could be at work through anything from songs to Starbucks cups to yoga. But why is it so easy for some to believe that the devil is more powerful than the divine? As if God's hands are tied while the devil is busy planning elaborate schemes of deception delivered in the form of cups of coffee.

I don't think God worries over Starbucks cups.

In addition to having suspicions about the stars, Christians have dismissed practices honoring the cycles of the moon and the celebrations thereof as "pagan" and dangerous, without regard for nuance. But is it true that there is no value in what the moon can reveal to us? As if God didn't create the moon, glorious, with a wisdom and power all its own. The apostle Paul says this himself: "The sun has one kind of glory, the moon has another kind of glory, and the stars have another kind of glory (but one star is different from another star in its glory)" (1 Cor. 15:41).

The moon is our closest celestial neighbor and, like the rest of the cosmos, one of our oldest relatives. Since early in their existence, humans have kept track of time using the cycles of the moon. The Hebrew calendar is lunar, looking to the moon and its phases in the night sky as a guide for the organization of the months.

We have long planned in accordance with the moon and made decisions in harmony with the seasons and constellations. And it didn't take long for us to realize that in addition to influencing our understanding of time, the lunar cycle has an effect on all kinds of life on earth. The moon's power holds sway on everything from bird migrations to the Great Barrier Reef to ocean tides pushing and pulling against the shore like a synchronized dance.

It's no wonder that many communities have tuned into the moon's cosmic energy, engaging in ceremonies honoring her wisdom. Throughout history, millions have gathered to sway and sing under her light, which waxes and wanes like the flow of our bodies in movement. Over time, however, we stopped looking to God's creation for guidance and instead were motivated by domination and productivity. Industrialization began ripping apart the human-nature bond, and instead of placing value in cycles and mysteries, we deemed them dangerous.

The psalmist attests that "God made the moon for the seasons" (Ps. 104:19). The moon and her gravitational pull are responsible for them. Much of the Western world takes the seasons for granted. The genetically modified foods that decorate our shelves and ruin our soil are evidence of our vain attempts at mastery over the land. We eat strawberries year-round, a luxury of the privileged. But for the ancient world and much of the globe today, seasons and sustenance go hand in hand. And the moon plays a central role in this.

In the Bible, for example, the seasons of the year are marked with special festivals. One such festival is Rosh Chodesh, the festival of the new moon, when the Israelites were to bring an offering to God. During biblical times, appointed messengers watched for the first visible appearance of this day, signaling to the rest of the community by igniting fires on the mountaintops and blowing trumpets in celebration.

Historically, God's people are a community gloriously tuned in to the rhythms and flow of the natural world and they have God to thank for this. Observing the new moon was the very first commandment given to the Jewish people (Exod. 12:1–2). New moon festivals were marked by social or family feasts and the ceasing of labor and trade. Fasting and mourning weren't allowed. This time signified new beginnings. It was a time of rest and celebration, a time of rejuvenation. Age-old farming practices, too, consider the time of the new moon, or waxing phases, as a time of fertility.

Have you ever looked at a full moon and thought about how marvelous it is that although it is over two hundred thousand miles away, our naked eye can see the battered surface where colliding asteroids and comets have left their mark? Generations past have looked upon the moon and wondered about her too. Future generations will do the same. She tethers us to our ancestors, beckoning us to remember. Acknowledging this celestial relative brings us back to our own bodies, our lineages, our lives.

The lens of the moon is the lens of change, mirroring the cycles of our lives. "Cycles of rest next to cycles of harvest lead to moments of embodiment—times spent clearing and reflecting."[1] The moon accompanies us wherever and however we are, inviting us into these creative processes inside and outside of ourselves.

●··●··●

It's dark outside as I write these words. I look out my window to get a glimpse of the moon for inspiration. I notice she is waxing, invisible. Would you believe it? A New Moon. I light a candle and remember the Israelites lighting their fires and blowing their trumpets as a call to celebrate newness. It is a time to engage in rest and rejuvenation. I think about the ways I can honor this sacred time like God commanded the Israelites to do in an invitation to be fully present, to remember, to feast, and to rest. In a world that emphasizes power, control, production, and greed, our moon asks us to pause and reflect. She coaxes us to connect.

In Genesis, God puts the moon in place to govern the night. Science confirms that the darker the night, the brighter she shines—not from her own light but from the reflection of the light of the sun across our solar system.

In the same way, the Talmud says that we don't see things as *they* are, we see them as *we* are. Perhaps the moon reminds us that the light we shine is a reflection of the divine.

Like her, we are mirrors.

- Have you ever sought to learn from the mystery of creation?
- How might the moon's phases guide you in more holistic living?

Day 31

The Prophets in Our Midst

Truly I tell you, anyone who will not receive the kingdom of
God like a little child will never enter it.

—Luke 18:17 (NIV)

When I was a kid, I befriended a back-door neighbor, a young girl
whose family had recently immigrated from Cuba. Our friendship
began shy and unsure, glancing over at each other while we played
alone across the yard, a silver chain-link fence protecting us from
each other. Each week, we'd inch our way closer and closer until one
magical day we found ourselves pressed right up against the fence,
sharing secrets through metal holes. After school, we'd both sprint to
the backyard to exchange drawings and stories and snacks. And then
one day it all changed: we finally got to play unencumbered. But it
wasn't the same. Without our fence—our rock-climbing wall, the pivot
point to our seesaw, our secret meeting place—the magic was lost.

I realize now that the chain-link fence we thought was hindering us
was the very thing our relationship thrived on. The world we invented
existed because of it. We created our Narnia, and once the enchant-
ment ended, we had no way to walk back into the magic.

Fences are usually seen as barriers. But for children, life contains
few barriers. It's the adults that build imaginary ones. A child's mind
is not yet hindered by the constraints of reality as adults see it; towels
become capes and brooms become scepters and suddenly children
are royalty. They look at stars and see holes punched into the sky.
Shadows become companions while on walks, and rocks become
chalk on pavement.

I recently learned that most children in infancy are considered "brilliant," but this changes as they get older—as adults begin teaching
them how the world "should" be, guiding or correcting them in a way

that robs them of their own innate wisdom and creativity. I've read the best gift you can give a child is refusing the urge to interrupt them when they're engaged in play.

Children are not burdened by the way things are *supposed* to work or what they're *supposed* to do: pots and pans double as instruments while pillows and blankets are forts waiting to be constructed.

If imagination is the color palette that Spirit speaks through, then our children are the paintbrushes.

Jesus said we must receive God's kingdom like a child. Some say this means we must lean into our helplessness and increase our dependence on God. Others say it means we must foster a sense of purity and innocence, but I think children have more to teach us than helplessness or innocence. Children are prophets.

When Jesus makes his appearance at the temple, shortly after he overturns the tables of money, children can be heard affirming him and crying out, "Hosanna to the Son of David!" (Matt. 21:15). This upsets the religious leaders and legal experts: "Do you hear what these children are saying?" they ask Jesus.

Jesus responds, "Haven't you ever read that from the mouths of babies God arranges perfect praises?" (Matt. 21:16, adapted, referencing Ps. 8:2).

It is the children's praises that counter the attacks hurled against Jesus—a subversive twist to the culture of hierarchy in which children are lowest in the social order. When many people doubted Jesus, it is the children who vocalized their support. It is *their* voices that minister to him. They understand the truth of Jesus's words and the weight of his actions with eyes that see what the adults will not. Their wisdom is prophetic.

Decolonizing our view of children—a view that stems from power, control, and hierarchy—can open us up to a new way of seeing the world and experiencing the divine, and it starts with seeing the children around us as spiritual teachers. In her book *Rewilding Motherhood*, Shannon Evans writes, "The more we say yes to the curiosity of our children, the more we realize we also have permission to say yes to our own curiosity: a permission slip that doubles as a ticket to a more awakened spiritual life."[1]

As the church body, our task is to envision new truths, to live into an "on earth as it is in heaven" reality. Unfortunately, as adults we tend to become conditioned to accept the world the way it is, forgetting the power we might hold to undo injustice and see our reality anew. This is why we need children in our midst, tiny individuals who are curious about what *could* be. It is our children who will set us free. Perhaps, then, we would do well to listen, instead of dismissing or silencing them.

Isaiah paints an otherworldly picture of this "on earth as it is in heaven" reality. His vision of the peaceable kingdom or "the new earth" hints at the restoration of humankind's role within creation. "The wolf will live with the lamb, and the leopard will lie down with the young goat; the calf and the young lion will feed together," he says. But what gets me is the last part: "and a little child will lead them" (Isa. 11:6). I cannot think of a more complete picture of a perfected world than a child leading wolves and leopards and lions—not with dominance, power, and coercion, as children and wild animals alike are led today— but with dignity, mutuality, and care. It is through the so-called weakest members of our human family that we have the most to learn about how to relate to the created world.

Such is God's kin-dom.

Perhaps, then, receiving it like a child means awakening our imagination and seeing the wonder and magic in our world. All people and things—a twig, a hairbrush, or a stranger on the street—have endless potential. But to enter into that world, we have to surrender our certainties and expectations. We must surrender the belief that we already know what everything is and is for and who or what we can learn from. We have to be willing to start over, assuming nothing, and learn to approach every created thing with awe: from the ant (see Prov. 6:6) to those overlooked and marginalized in our society. This takes an incredible amount of humility.

"Who is the greatest in the kingdom of heaven?" the disciples ask Jesus. He calls over a child and says, "Those who humble themselves like this little child will be the greatest in the kingdom of heaven" (Matt. 18:1, 4).

To be like a child is to get over ourselves and our perceived "right" beliefs, views, and understandings. It is to break from the norm and reimagine a new world and a new reality: one where wardrobes are portals to fantasy lands and chain-link fences are pivot points for see-saws, where wolves live with lambs and ants are our greatest teachers; and where injustice has absolutely no place in the house of God.

- Reflect on the lessons children have taught you. How have they helped you envision a new reality?

Day 32

The Cardinal Directions

You will spread out to the west, east, north, and south. Every family of earth will be blessed because of you and your descendants.

—Genesis 28:14

I know the sun rises in the east and sets in the west. But tell me to go north, and I'll look at you like you're speaking a foreign language. That's because the language of directions is not one I speak eloquently. Thanks to modern technologies that make our lives easier, many of us lack the basic directional skills that were vital to the survival of our ancestors.

I remember the first time I held a map and a compass in my hand and was guided in the practice of orienting myself. I realized how helpless I was without this skill. Somewhere in the Rocky Mountains, I was entirely at the mercy of the elements. But the gift of simply knowing where I came from and where I was headed was empowering. It changed my experience, giving me a sense of agency and even connection with the natural world. It's as if we were speaking a language of our own. While I didn't become an expert in orienteering, those who showed me the way taught me that this practice is a sacred one.

Across Native cultures, the four cardinal directions (east, south, west, and north) are imbued with meaning and spiritual significance. In Native American spirituality, specifically, the Medicine Wheel, sometimes called the Wheel of Life, symbolizes life's cycle and offers guidance for living as it moves in a clockwise direction without a beginning or end, aligning with the forces of nature—like gravity and the rising and setting of the sun.[1]

The practice of honoring the cardinal directions was disrupted in the Americas when colonizers sought to end Indigenous practices and disregarded the knowledge that had guided their communities for thousands of years.

But even the Bible repeatedly references the four cardinal directions. This is why many have found value in honoring them. Doing so honors "the four quadrants of the earth from where distinct people hail, with each being equal and integral to the existence of the next."[2] The four sacred directions remind us of our connectedness to each other and the earth, offering us lessons that correlate to the cycle of life. Like our seasons of life, each direction is to be understood not as separate or isolated but as part of an interdependent system.

●··●··●

East. As the direction related to the rising of the sun, the east has long been thought of as the main point of orientation. In the life cycle, it represents birth. In the Bible, it is mentioned in Genesis as the direction where the garden of Eden and its entrance were located (2:8; 3:24). First Adam and Eve, and then eventually the whole human race (11:2–4), head eastward.[3] For the prophets, God's intervention and salvation from oppressive empires often came from the east (Ezek. 11:23; Rev. 16:12).

Christine Valters Paintner notes that in the Christian tradition, the east became tied to the resurrection (Matt. 24:27), with many churches building their altars facing in this direction. Cemeteries, too, often orient east so people can be buried with their feet eastward so that when they are resurrected, they rise facing God.[4]

In Native traditions, east represents spring—new beginnings and the dawning of a new day. Birds in flight are associated with the east. When people speak words of affirmation, they might be offered in this direction with the intention that they will fly and soar toward Spirit. Gratitude, for example, is often sent east "for the chance to learn every day, to start anew."[5]

South. The south symbolizes great abundance in ancient traditions. It is the direction where the sun is at its highest point in the sky, representing fire and passion. In the life cycle, it reflects our childhood—full of energy, curiosity, and eagerness for life. South is connected to the season of summer in which all creation is teeming with life and growth. It is where "the green that covers the world," as Robin Wall Kimmerer writes, "is carried on the warm winds." She notes that in Indigenous tradition, the life of all things is believed to come from the south, and when people die, this is the direction to which they return.[6]

In the Bible, south is the direction from which God appeared to Moses (Deut. 33:2) and represents God's right hand—a place or position of strength, abundance, and blessing.

West. In the Bible, the west relates to darkness since it is the direction of the sunset (Ps. 104:19). It is also correlated with water. In Hebrew, there are a few different words that are used for "west." One of these is the word *yam* which also translates to "sea," and the word *acharon* can also be translated "last," as in the last place along the horizon where the sun is located before setting in the evening.[7] These notions can also be found in Native cultures. The Aztecs believed that the goddess of water resided in the west, and in Native American traditions the west represents the season of autumn and "the final harvest as the end of a cycle."[8] In the life cycle, west corresponds with adulthood, and the notion of figuring things out and exercising wisdom. Like the fall, it represents a time of preparation.

In Judaism, the west points toward the presence of God, where the Holy of Holies resided, and is the direction the Israelites crossed in order to enter into the Promised Land. God traveled with them to Israel in the west, pointing them to a path of restoration and unity with the divine.[9]

North. The Hebrew word for north is *tzafon,* which means "hidden" and is associated with darkness, gloom, and the unknown. It can also be defined as "gazing" or "looking out" and refers to the name of a high mountain that resides north of Israel.

In the Cherokee tradition, the north represents the dark of winter: the season of waiting and surviving. It reminds us to be patient with the changing of the seasons.[10] Like the natural world that is dormant during this time, the north is a place of introspection and mystery. Similarly, in the life cycle, north is the place of the elder who has journeyed through each direction. "Looking out," they are now able to guide and initiate others in the mystery of this world. The animal of the north is the buffalo, which lays down its life to nourish and sustain others. In the Bible, the north is the place of God's celestial dwelling (Isa. 14:13), a guiding light.

● ·· ● ·· ●

"Where can I go from your Spirit?" asks the psalmist (Ps. 139:7). As a kid, when I carried an image of God as an angry, old judge, this thought terrified me. But liberation can be found in the idea of God as a Spirit you cannot hide from, because we know we also have a constant companion who journeys alongside us in the cycles of our lives. God's presence is like a bird in flight soaring toward the east where new life emerges, or a fierce protector at our right hand—flaming the southern fires of passion and curiosity of our youth. A boundless God as vast as the sea in the west, intimate and present in the wilderness, a place we find ourselves in seasons of preparation. Even in the cold winters of the north, in the midst of the darkness, I know I can look out and find the divine, my guiding light, that nourishes and sustains me so that I may do the same for others.

> If I go up to the heavens, you are there;
> if I make my bed in the depths, you are there.
> If I rise on the wings of the dawn,
> if I settle on the far side of the sea,
> even there your hand will guide me,
> your right hand will hold me fast. (Ps. 139:8–10 NIV)

To honor the sacred directions is to engage in "a form of prayer containing a map of that which constitutes our human condition and the powers of the natural world," writes Lara Medina.[11] And it is to this natural world that we are bound. Acknowledging both its limits and its grandeur within the four sacred directions gifts us this reality like a mercy new each morning.

Making it a practice to orient ourselves from wherever we are honors our place in relation to the world—both spiritually and physically. It acknowledges where we are in the cycle of our lives and how Spirit might be moving among us. It serves as a focal point from which our being and knowing radiates. From north to south to east to west we remember our ancestors who found life and meaning in this long-honored tradition, holding our communities together for generations and generations.[12]

THE
FEMININE

Day 33

Pachamama

During dinner, a woman came in with a vase made of alabaster
and containing very expensive perfume of pure nard. She broke
open the vase and poured the perfume on [Jesus's] head.

—Mark 14:3

I can imagine a time long before people began to kill each other, before
bodies were bought and sold and land and women became property,
the Sun Children lived among the mountains. They sang and inhaled
the breath of life that came from the wind they could not see, and
when they felt it, they danced. When they danced the trees moved too,
swaying along with them, for all their energy was connected.

The Sun Children understood themselves as part of a larger ecosystem in which everything had a place and a purpose. This they called
ayni (reciprocity). And with a spirit of ayni, they let their thanksgiving
be a chorus toward the cosmos, lifting their throats and exhaling love,
knowing they would receive it in return.

They offered borrowed gifts to their Earth Mother, gifts she first
gave to them: flowers, leaves, water, seeds. They planted their gardens
in rows and patterns that looped up and down slopes and around
valleys and ridges, creating a tapestry that clothed and cared for their
mother. Her name was Pachamama. She provided for them, and they
provided for her.

●··●··●

In most early civilizations, people believed that the creator of all
things was female. In Incan mythology, Pachamama is a deity of fertility also known as Mother Nature or Earth Mother. Pachamama
lived in the mountains and presided over the harvests. The Incans

held daily rituals honoring her. They showed their appreciation by whispering their gratitude and handing small handfuls of cornmeal back to the earth.

After the Spanish conquered the Incans, Pachamama was replaced with the Virgin Mary.

When patriarchal religions like Judaism and Christianity entered the scene, religions with female deities were soon suppressed.[1] Before long, violence and domination reshaped societies into militarized powers and God became a male warrior and ruler.[2] This continued through the colonial era, which marked the transformation of labor. Soon, power centered "around the axis of capital and the world market," leading to land ownership and increased exploitation.[3] Land and bodies—particularly female bodies—were simply commodities to domesticate, own, tame, and control.

This time in history also gave rise to a dualistic way of looking at the world, particularly in regard to bodies, which were now seen as hindrances to spiritual and intellectual pursuits. Patriarchal spirituality associated women with both the body and nature—two things that had to be transcended in order to be "like God." Thus, the oppression and suppression of women and nature was made a sacred pursuit.[4]

The domination and exploitation of women and nature by Western industrial civilization were mutually reinforcing because women were characterized as carnal, earthly, chaotic, unpredictable, irrational, and subjective. Men, on the other hand, associated with mind and reason, were characterized as rational, ordered, spiritual, intellectual, and objective. And since they controlled the public domain, men were thus capable of directing the use and development of both women and nature.

This is precisely the reason why we cannot talk about the earth, our spirituality, or the body without engaging the feminine. We cannot be free without acknowledging that the domination of women and the domination and degradation of nature are intricately connected— consequences of patriarchy, colonialism, and capitalism. But poor, rural women suffer disproportionate harms. Environmental problems that arise from exploitation of the land affect women of color the most. Deforestation and water pollution require the most marginalized among us to walk twice as far to gather resources, putting them in danger and making it harder for them to feed their families.[5] Similarly, in the United States, toxic waste landfills are often located in Black and Latinx urban communities, contaminating the water and soil in these areas and putting vulnerable populations at risk. As womanist theologian Emilie Townes writes, dumpsites such as this are "contemporary versions of lynching a whole people."[6]

Making the connection between the feminine and ecology is essential for the liberation of both.

● ● ● ● ● ● ●

There's a story in the Gospels, right before Jesus is betrayed, in which a woman enters Simon's house, a place previously associated with healing (Matt. 1:29). Here, Jesus is reclining with his friends when the woman begins pouring expensive ointment on his head. This upsets those present, but Jesus defends her. "I tell you the truth," he says, "that wherever in the whole world this good news is announced, what she's done will also be told in memory of her" (Mark 14:9).

Sermons I've heard preached about this story have often highlighted the woman's adoration, her devotion so strong that she spends all her money (a year's wages, they say) on this oil to anoint Jesus. And I agree; her sacrifice is certainly admirable. But more notable to me is her empathy and also her audacity. Not only was the dinner party this woman crashed a male-dominated space, but ointments like the one she used were often gendered, appropriated and used by men to heal ailments primarily of the head or the brain—the "manly" parts of the body.[7]

This is significant given the context. Jesus knew his death was imminent. In fact, only two days later, he tells the disciples of the despair this caused him: "It's as if I'm dying," he tells them (Mark 14:34). Perhaps the woman had some insight into the anguish Jesus was experiencing. Maybe she was so attuned to him that she sensed it. Or maybe she knew what Jesus was going through personally. Disregarding what's "appropriate" in this space, the woman crosses culturally and socially gendered boundaries to offer Jesus this healing ointment in order to ease his mental distress.

The ointment, too, has a deeper meaning. It acts as a symbol of the earth's gifts that provide healing to all—including Jesus. It is a gift "graciously given by the earth to the woman who, in turn, pours it out generously to give healing compassion to Jesus as he faces into his death," notes theologian Elaine Wainwright.[8] Her audacious actions offer Jesus both "earth's healing resource and women's healing power."[9] But the disciples are insulted. They fail to recognize the deep pain and anxiety Jesus is experiencing, and they dismiss her action as *waste*. How dare she be so inappropriate, unpredictable, and irrational? They disregard the healing this woman holds in her body, in her hands—one that comes from the earth herself. But Jesus not only recognizes it, he affirms it. He says it will *never* be forgotten. This gift has prepared his body for burial and is imparted to him through an intimate, audacious, empathetic, and sacred act.

In this story, both Jesus and the woman cross boundaries as the healer becomes the healed and the one who would typically need the healing assumes the position of healer.

The story of the woman who anoints Jesus communicates a deeper truth in the link between women and nature that has been distorted by patriarchy as a way to exploit both: women are healers. As the inventors of agriculture and the primary food-gatherers, women are nurturers and life-givers. While these characteristics have been used to subjugate us, it's important we reclaim the power and life that emanate from our beings. It was by experiencing these qualities and characteristics in women "that early humans made the image of the female the first personification of the divine, the source of all life."[10] Still today, women find themselves responding to their communities' needs when lands are destroyed by war and the soil degraded through unsustainable industrial farming practices.

While the feminine has long been associated with the healing of the land and the healing of people, the effects of patriarchy on the land and on women feel almost impossible to reverse.

"What's the hope?" a colleague asked in class one day as we reflected on this.

"Resistance is the hope," my professor responded, and I think about that every day as I nurture the world around me.

●·●·●

No matter how we identify as people in this world, we must lean into the feminine in each of us. As humans made in the divine image, tuning into our nurturing, emotive, and embodied qualities is the crucial first step toward the liberation of ourselves and our planet. And like the woman who heals in the Gospel of Matthew, we must continue to transgress boundaries, resist cultural norms, and press on toward healing for the sake of our children and their children.

This starts with daily practices of taking care of the land and people around us. We learn to cultivate and to mother. We pour small handfuls of cornmeal or seeds, and we whisper words of gratitude to the earth that sustains us.

We resist patriarchy—domination, exploitation, and hierarchy—so that we may heal.

- In what ways are we tapping into the feminine qualities in us and in nature and in the divine in order to heal?
- What does resistance to domination, exploitation, and hierarchy look like in your day-to-day life?

Day 34

The Real Thing

✳

You will conceive and give birth to a son . . .

—Luke 1:31

"I'm scared," I said as I felt my insides quivering. It was time. I had spent the last ten months preparing myself for this moment. I read that when people in birth begin to "transition"—that is, when the cervix has reached full dilation and the baby is about to descend—we panic. While I knew it was a common response and it meant my body was getting ready to give birth, I was still surprised at how terrifying it felt to have no control of what your body is about to do. "I can't do this," I told my doula with a trembling voice.

She responded, "Your body is doing what it's meant to do. Trust her."

I suddenly found myself in the tub with my child's head crowning, visible outside of my body. With every contraction, I heard a sound erupt from inside me that I had never heard before: a roar, a groan elicited from the core of my being. It was primal.

I read once that giving birth is like flipping a light switch off and then back on and finding yourself on the moon, and that's exactly what it was like for me: an otherworldly experience. I've never felt more out-of-body and embodied at exactly the same time. It was wholly material and wholly spiritual, a vivid reminder of how intertwined the two truly are. Aren't the most sacred things in life this way?

Christmas rolled around a few months after my daughter was born, and as can be expected, I no longer saw the birth of Christ the same way. The image of the nativity as we're used to seeing it stands out to me: the figure of a clean and swaddled Christ, animals lying peacefully nearby, Mary fully dressed and kneeling by the baby, and guests and gifts and twinkling stars decorating the scene.

You'd think this image, meant to portray peace and hope, would be calming. But that first Advent as a new mother, the nativity scene brought me only angst. I've learned that most renderings are sanitized this way. The Christian empire, specifically, sells us images of what divinity is *supposed* to be, what a life of faith *should* look like, but like the nativity scene, it's often a far cry from the real thing.

I've often said that the Bible is a book written by men, for men. Throughout the centuries most of its interpreters and preachers have been men as well. It's no surprise then, that the story of the incarnation—and it's rendering and interpretations thereafter—would glide over the messy realities of pregnancy and labor. Indeed, we're told about the politics requiring Joseph to register in his hometown, about the shepherds keeping watch, and about heavenly hosts of angels celebrating, but we hear nothing of the blood, the nakedness, the primal groans, the fear, the strength and power of the human body, the first-time shrieks of new life bursting into the world.

But what could an *edited* story of incarnation possibly say about the sacred? "It is as though the truth of birth is too secular for Immanuel," writes Sarah Bessey.[1] Perhaps this is where we received our first antiseptic views of holiness, from a sterilized story of incarnation far removed from its reality. We've come to understand the concept of holiness as uncontaminated from the realities of the world, but is this truly the story of divinity? The story of God entering into our grief, our sorrows, our joys?

Like so many renderings of the narratives in Scripture, the birth of Jesus has been domesticated and dulled to make it more palatable. But there's something subversively fleshly and carnal about Mary birthing God and her role as an active agent in the messy, material, and imminent.

I wonder, *What was it like for Mary to birth God?* What was it like to feel God squirm and settle as he pressed against her organs? She probably got short of breath and had trouble finding a comfortable position for sleep at night. She might have wondered if her skin could possibly stretch any more to contain her son and all he will become, yet each day her body did what it was designed to do.

Was she scared? Did she stay up with anxiety wondering if she'd survive childbirth, as delivery-related deaths were not uncommon in the ancient world? Did she panic like I did as Jesus's body began to burst through her? Did she roar and groan, her primal instincts taking over? How long was she in labor; how strong were her contractions? Did she give birth standing up, squatting, or on all fours? Did the smell of the stable make her nauseous?

What was it like for her to suckle God at her breast? Did her nipples crack and bleed those early days of breastfeeding? Did tears roll down her cheeks every time Jesus tried to latch?

The story goes that Mary and Joseph took the baby to get dedicated in the temple in Jerusalem (Luke 2:22–23). This required several miles of walking. How did her postpartum body handle that? How long did she have to recover before getting on the road? Did it hurt to sit? How long did she have postpartum bleeding? Did her surging hormones make her cry about anything and everything? Did she get postpartum depression?

We talk about Jesus's body being broken for us, but we don't talk enough about how Mary's body was broken for him.

This matters because a broken, refugee, brown, female, naked, stretched, hormonal, marginalized body is how divinity entered this world and where divinity still makes itself most known today. "I care that God became human not through a man's sperm, but a woman's womb," writes KJ Ramsey. "I care that female bodies, disabled bodies, and marginalized bodies continue to be the battleground where much of the church most reduces the story of Love into mere words."[2]

The nativity scene, like much of Western theology, is far removed from the very bloody and very raw and very human process of birth. But these are the kinds of things that make up our faith: the naked, the primal, even the offensive. And while Mary's story turned out the way she'd hope it would—with a newborn child in her arms—not all stories turn out that way. What the nativity scene as we're used to seeing it fails to show us is that our faith is made of that too: the sadness, the questions, the longing, the despair, the anger. Encompassed within the birth of Jesus is the deeply difficult and deeply beautiful, the sacred and the profane, the spiritual and the material. Like our lives, it was fleshly and carnal—and it was also holy.

It is in *this* space where we not only find and experience the divine, but it is in *this* space where the divine became human and dwelt among us.

The Christian empire might try to sell us images of what God is like, of what faith and life and spirituality are *supposed* to look like—clean, orderly, and controlled—but the raw, unedited birth of Jesus reminds us that rejecting these images gives way to experiencing the real thing in all its messy glory.

The Power of the Erotic

✦

My own vineyard is mine to give.
—Song of Songs 8:12 (NIV)

I held my first packet of condoms in my outstretched palm like a disease. "Just in case," Mom told me, but it sounded more like a question. I was leaving for college the next day, four hundred miles from home, and it was one way my mom offered herself to me like a sacrifice, praying to God her gesture would be seen not as an invitation to use them but as a way to let me know she could be trusted if ever I did. Having raised me as a single mother for a large part of my childhood, Mom did the best she could with the resources she had to make me feel supported as I navigated all the uncomfortable feelings and experiences that come with growing up. She wasn't perfect, but she also wasn't naive about those experiences, and that was a gift. Regardless of her efforts, however, machismo was in the air I breathed, burrowed into my culture like a parasite.

Later, when I would embrace evangelicalism, purity culture would swallow me whole, and I would take on a shame as an adult that was never mine to bear. I would feel guilty for the confidence I felt in who I was as a woman. Mom taught me that my body was mine, and I was in control of it; I needed only to exercise wisdom and compassion for myself. It was the church that taught me a different message, that my sexuality was dangerous—not from but against God—something that needed to be hidden and contained, buried so deep that it would cause a chasm within me.

●‥●‥●‥●

The Song of Songs has proved a difficult, albeit intriguing, book to interpret due to its provocative nature. A read through the poem offers us a look into the longings of the human experience. And it does so in ways that might surprise us. When we approach the Bible this way, willing for it to speak to us about the depths and nuances of being human, we might find freedom from the confines of a colonized spirituality.

I think the Song of Songs serves as a guide in this respect.

Within its kaleidoscope of similes and metaphors, we are met with the voice of the Shulamite—the unusually dominant female voice spotlighted throughout the poem. She is a woman who projects a self-empowerment rarely seen in female biblical characters.

"I am black and beautiful," she declares in her first monologue at the opening of the book (Song 1:5).

Amen.

Unashamed and unapologetic, the Shulamite's presence is undeniable. Never called a wife nor found under the authority of a father or husband, the Shulamite reads as someone free from the constraints of patriarchal tradition, free from the boundaries of marriage. Neither is she expected to bear children, relieving her from the confines of reproductive duty. In this way, she is free to explore her desires. Acting on her own impulse, the Shulamite initiates a romantic relationship with a sense of boldness. She is honest about her sexual yearnings—they are not hidden, nor is she reserved about them.[1]

The Shulamite is not your traditional biblical character, nor is the sphere of love and eroticism she inhabits with her lover a traditional biblical social structure. Throughout the poem, the masculine and feminine roles given to the lovers resist conventional norms. For example, many of the Song's images and metaphors are derived from the military, as the world of the Bible was a world often filled with violence, warfare, and militarized conquest. As such, anything related to the military in the ancient world was primarily associated with men. In a subversive reversal, the military language used in the Song is specifically prescribed to the woman, without exception. This reversal of gender stereotypes is shocking and unexpected—especially since the same is true for the man. In the text, he is likened to a gazelle, an animal associated in the ancient world with femininity.[2]

This erotic poem is revolutionary in more ways than one, beckoning us to consider how the divine might be pushing conventional boundaries. Indeed, we might find liberation here.

Perhaps one of the most moving details about the Shulamite is how she experiences her own becoming: how she shifts, changes, and grows more into herself as the poem progresses. We experience a taste of this when she proclaims her Blackness, but immediately after she also confesses that she has neglected her own vineyards (Song 1:6). And isn't this such a refreshing admission? For women, specifically, how many of us have been conditioned to neglect our own vineyards, our sexuality, ourselves? The effects are such that women can become strangers to their own bodies.

But the Shulamite woman offers us a new perspective. From the first chapter to the last, she shifts from neglecting her vineyard to asserting, "My own vineyard is mine to give" (Song 8:12 NIV). By the end of the Song, she "is no more subjected to the prescriptions of patriarchy, nor to the whims and desires of those around her; she is her own person," says womanist scholar Abi Doukhan. She steps into her agency, deciding how, when, and to whom she will offer herself—recovering ownership of her own body and her sexuality, "her vineyard." It is under no one else's authority but her own.[3]

It is when a woman has a sense of herself—her desires and her longings—that she's able to shift the power dynamics previously in place and lead her community "to the dawn of a new era."[4] Here is true equality and partnership in relationships, including sexual relationships where women have most often been at the receiving end of abuse and exploitation. Audre Lorde speaks of women needing to reconnect to this power within themselves, the power of the erotic. Lorde explains that this power is a resource that lies in "a deeply female and spiritual plane," and goes on to assert that women's erotic power has historically been suppressed, alienating us from our own bodies and robbing us of energy within ourselves. Inevitably, this causes us to distrust the power that rises from our deepest knowledge—our embodied wisdom.[5] Thus, if we want to see true equality in our society, women must be in touch with the power of the erotic. We must be awakened to who we are and what we want.

But the erotic is not necessarily sexual. In fact, Willie James Jennings writes that the erotic has been so commodified and sexualized that Christians have turned away from it in fear that it signifies moral failing and sin. Jennings puts forth a different view of eroticism, one "formed in the body of Jesus and the protocols of breaking, sharing, touching, tasting and seeing the goodness of God."[6]

Erotic power speaks to our capacity for intimacy and involves the union of body, spirit, reason, and passion. It is "the power of our primal interrelatedness," writes theologian Rita Nakashima Brock. It involves all of who we are in relationships of self-awareness, vulnerability, and caring.[7] The power of the erotic speaks to the power of our deepest belonging, our tetheredness to one another and, as Lorde says, the measure of our deepest joy.[8]

Perhaps this is the gift the Shulamite gives us: the permission to tap into the power of our sexuality and the power of the erotic within us. Doing so might enhance connection and diminish fragmentation to ourselves, to each other, and to the divine, thereby leading us to experience the truest measure of belonging within the family of God. Only then, when we are free of the hierarchy that leads to exploitation and abuse, might we experience the joy and liberation offered to us in the sensual, intuitive, intimate, and emotional body of Christ.

- How might the power of the erotic reconnect you to yourself, to God, and to community?
- How might Song of Songs as a whole challenge your ideas of sexuality?

The Breasted One

✴

Your stature is like that of the palm,
and your breasts like clusters of fruit.
I said, "I will climb the palm tree;
I will take hold of its fruit."

—Song of Songs 7:7–8 (NIV)

I sit to write about breasts with a clogged milk duct on my right one, pain emanating and throbbing, reminding me that my body is fragile and tender. I alternate between a warm and a cold compress, keeping my breast free of restrictions so that it may heal. A shift is happening in me as I learn to treat my breasts with dignity, nurturing and taking care of them so that they may nurture and take care of my child. This is new for me.

As is the case with many women, my breasts have often caused me shame. I was embarrassed by their first appearance while in middle school, returning from eighth-grade summer break to whispers in the hallways.

"Did you stuff your bra?" a classmate asked. I didn't know what she meant, but my cheeks burned hot and so did my insecurity. As a result, I made my mom buy me new PE shirts two sizes too big. I retained my embarrassment in my twenties and thirties, when it seemed to me they didn't meet societal standards for what women's breasts *should* look like. Too big? Too small? Not perky enough? It seems we can never get it right.

But breaking free from these standards is recognizing that like the rest of the female body, our breasts are dynamic. They respond to the world around us like few other organs. When my daughter's sleep habits changed, for example, so did the amount of milk they produced to match her needs. My breasts provide food, but they also regulate themselves, picking up cues from the environment. This is why breasts are the most tumor-prone organ in the human body, according to writer Florence Williams. They absorb pollutants and act as the indicator or predictor of changing health.[1]

With nearly three hundred thousand cases of breast cancer a year, our breasts might also trigger emotional responses from those who have been probed and prodded, undergone chemotherapy, mastectomies, and more. Still others carry around a grief inexplicable from walking alongside those who have lost the fight with this disease.

"Breasts carry the burden of the mistakes we have made in our stewardship of the planet," says Williams, "and they alert us to them if we know how to look."[2] Our bodies tell us important things we need to know. Familiarizing ourselves with them might awaken a new wisdom in ourselves and in the world.

●··●··●

In previous times, female deities were often depicted with breasts—sometimes many of them—as they were associated with love, nourishment, and fertility. Even certain male deities were shown with breast-like appendices. As Shannon Evans notes, "Fertility statues were used to pray not only to receive the blessing of children but also for the fertility of the land—as well as a way to honor sex and love as an end in themselves."[3]

Before the female body was hypereroticized in the culture at large, the early church fathers regularly referenced breasts in their theological writings. Augustine refers to the disciples "drink[ing] at the fountain of the Lord's breast." Elsewhere, he said that "Mother Church" feeds us from her breasts which are "the two testaments of the divine Scriptures."[4] Still others like Irenaeus and Clement of Alexandria speak of Christ as milk coming from the Father's breasts. Saint Ephrem, a fourth-century doctor of the Church called Jesus the "Breast of Life," and preacher John Chrysostom compared Christ to a woman who "nurtures her offspring with her own blood and milk."[5]

While the early church fathers understood the value of breasts, most likely due to Scripture's frequent mention of them, they often went only as far as highlighting their role in providing food. The Bible certainly talks about breasts this way, but they don't only serve this purpose. Both God and Israel are depicted as having them (Ezek. 16:7). In fact, one of God's names, El Shaddai, means "The Breasted One"—a name hotly contested by some male interpreters. In most places that El Shaddai is located in Scripture, it's usually found alongside the command to be fruitful and multiply.[6] In Isaiah, full breasts represent refreshment (Isa. 66:10–11). They are a source of enjoyment and satisfaction (Song 7:3, 7–8) as well as contentment and comfort (Ps. 131:2). Solomon advises his sons to honor the wife of their youth and "let her breasts intoxicate you" (Prov. 5:19).

The bottom line is that in Scripture breasts are seen not as a source of shame but an integral part of the body. They nurture and give sustenance, but they are also to be enjoyed. There are no parts of our bodies that are void of value in all the intimate and complex ways we live out our humanity.

●··●··●

I took over the leadership of a high school group for girls when their regular mentor was diagnosed with breast cancer. I'd lead the weekly group sessions while she focused on healing. Maria joined us one Thursday, her body weakened but her spirit unchanged. That night, she told us about how during these trying times she felt God holding her, her head tucked into God's chest. "Right here," she said, pointing to her own chest just above the place her skin was beginning to heal, a scar forming at the site that her breast tissue had been removed.

I thought of Maria years later when I was first discovering Julian of Norwich. Sitting on the floor of my living room, I cried as her words swept over me: "The Mother may lay the child tenderly to her breast, but our tender Mother, Jesus, He may homely lead us into His blessed breast."[7] This is the experience Maria knew so intimately.

I grew up estranged from my father, so I could never relate to fatherly metaphors for God. How could I *feel* and *know* God as a father? But Julian's words about a mother, a God who nurtures and nourishes her young from the breast felt entirely present and meaningful. They awakened something in me. Knowing God as mother meant connecting with God in an intimate way that knowing God as father never had and, frankly, never could for me. To fathom God having feminine features, breasts—yes, like my own—whether they nurse or not, profoundly shifted my relationship with the divine and showed me that God meets us exactly how and where we need to be met. What an indelible realization, to know that God takes on the image of God's creation.

This imagery moves me even now as I tend to my own breast, massaging this lump that has formed from clogged milk. I feel a new connection to this integral part of my body, these handiworks of the divine that hold their own form of wisdom, knowing that despite how society might try to convince me otherwise, they are of value—worthy of dignity and respect.

- Is there a part of your body you have neglected to learn about? How might you come to know it better?
- How has a God with feminine features ministered to you in the past? How might you connect more intimately with the divine feminine?

Day 37

Primary Issues

⭐

Jesus stood up and said to her, "Woman, where are they? Is there
no one to condemn you?"

—John 8:10

"Your desire will be for your husband, and he will rule over you,"
he said, flexing his right bicep under a dark blue suit, "because he's
stronger."

My heart sank into my stomach. *Because he's stronger?* I wondered,
confused. I didn't know a lot of things about the so-called curse in
Genesis 3 back then, but the notion of men ruling over women due
to physical strength made absolutely no sense. I knew a lot of women
who were physically stronger than plenty of men.

I waited to hear more, but my professor had already moved on. I
looked around at a room full of men. No one batted an eye at what
we had just heard. For them, this interpretation meant nothing, but
to me it meant everything.

It was the first week of my Old Testament course, and I was looking
forward to wrestling with Genesis 3 alongside people who I thought
took the Bible seriously. I admit, my understanding of what "taking
the Bible seriously" means has since changed drastically. I've learned
that when dominant readings of the Bible don't cause you to question your humanity, when your privilege and power leave you with
no vested interest or skin in the game, when there are no high stakes
for you, then it becomes easy to glide past interpretations like these
without giving them much thought. You are free to ignore or dismiss
them because it means nothing in your day-to-day life. But for the rest
of us, texts like these and how they're read can feel like life or death;
they can affect how we're treated, how we perceive our own passions,
callings, or vocations, and even how we engage in the world.

While I don't waste my time or my breath anymore trying to convince men that women should be regarded as equals, I do not consider the issues of women in Scripture as "secondary." The disregard with which my professor approached the topic of subordination in class is part of the reason why abuse is continually perpetuated in Christian spaces.

● ● ● ● ● ●

One passage in Genesis is often overlooked because it's, well, utterly bizarre. It's found in chapter 6 and occurs just before the story of Noah, when God destroys the earth and its inhabitants through a catastrophic flood. The reason God decides to do so, according to the text, is because "humanity had become thoroughly evil" (v. 5). We are not told what this means, but we are told that God regretted making humankind and decides to start over by wiping out everything under the sky that breathes (v. 17). The text doesn't specify what corruption people were engaging in on earth, but it does detail the unusual presence of giants—Nephilim, they're called. It says these supernatural beings roamed the earth and fathered children with mortal women.

I often heard that the sexual relations the divine beings had with human daughters was a major aspect of the evil that was happening in these early days. Because of the complex nature of this text, I assume, not much more was said, and I didn't ask too many questions or offer many objections. The Bible often felt inaccessible due to the complex nature of many of its passages. Because of its difficulties, some who teach from the Bible either engage in a sort of theological gymnastics in order to make sense of it or they dismiss these passages—insisting we simply trust that God is good despite how troubling they might be. Oftentimes, this results in a lack of deep engagement with its more disturbing aspects.[1]

I know better now than to withhold my questions or set aside my objections.

I wonder if perhaps so many of us have become wary of the Bible because we've been told to love God with all our heart, mind, soul, and strength while simultaneously being expected to disengage from these same things when reading it. In evangelical circles, many of us were trained to zip right through stories of conquest, sexualized violence, and mindless slaughter with dispassionate acceptance. But loving God with every part of our being requires us to bring all of ourselves to the table—even and especially our doubts, questions, disagreements, grievances, frustrations, and traumas.

This is why years later I began to wrestle with these difficulties in Scripture, asking questions about texts that forced me to linger in the discomfort. After I graduated from seminary, the #MeToo and #Church-Too movements started gaining traction, and suddenly so many things that I had never really questioned in Scripture began demanding more of my attention. I reread Genesis 6 one day and something peculiar caught my eye. The narrative wasn't as simple as human daughters and divine beings having sex. For the first time I noticed what the text *actually* says: "The divine beings saw how beautiful these human women were, so *they married the ones they chose*" (Gen. 6:2, emphasis mine).

For the first time the thought crossed my mind, perhaps it was this that made God regret making humankind: that the Nephilim had objectified and taken women for themselves—whomever they chose—seemingly without their consent. Perhaps *that* was enough corruption to make God want to start all over. I dare to believe that God takes sexual abuse that seriously. Noticing this detail in the text sparked a new journey of discovery and asking the hard and uncomfortable questions when it comes to sexualized violence (and conquest, among other things) and the Bible.

Oftentimes it is the overspiritualizing of passages that can make us miss simple, profound points, like the fact that God hates the domination of any person over the other. No theological gymnastics or dismissal required.

In John 8, there is a story about a woman accused of adultery who suffers shame and humiliation as a tool to accuse Jesus. She is subjected to abuse to further the cause of his enemies, who wish to see whether he will defy the law that asserts she must be stoned (John 8:6). He tells those who haven't sinned to go ahead and throw the first one. Everyone walks away and Jesus tells her he doesn't condemn her.

What might our world look like if we were encouraged to linger in the presence of injustice—whether in the Bible or in our midst—the way Jesus lingered with this woman? He didn't dismiss nor did he overspiritualize. Doing likewise might allow us to engage the Bible and the world in authentic, meaningful, and life-changing ways.

It was lingering here that made me realize that perhaps this narrative is less about judgment or forgiveness than it is about challenging the notion of the dispensability of women. Perhaps Jesus was not as concerned about being right as he was about ensuring that women used as objects for manipulation are given dignity.

As part of my spiritual practice these days, I do not quickly move past passages in which violence is enacted, particularly on women. I do not simply keep reading, accepting it for what it is and, thus, emotionally distancing myself from the discomfort of injustice. I refuse to disengage my own conscience or intuition, given to me by God, that tells me what's right and what's wrong. Instead, I linger, the same way Jesus did.

Only then am I able to truly love my God and my neighbor with every part of my being: my heart, mind, soul, and strength.

- How might you confront injustice in your circle of relationships? In your community? On a societal level?

Day 38

Uncontrollable Flows

✳

But Jesus said, "Someone touched me; I know that power has
gone out from me."

—Luke 8:46

I sit down at my desk to type, shifting in discomfort as the all too familiar twinges of pain tug at my uterus. I resist the urge to numb it with painkillers—at least for now. I go to the bathroom and look down; I'm bleeding. It's been almost six months since my uterus sustained and brought forth life, and now the cycle has begun again—on the day I sit to write these words.

Perhaps my body, in all her wisdom, knew.

I got my first period on September 11, 2001, the same day the World Trade Center towers disintegrated into the ground like sand. It was a strange and uncertain day for everyone, but strange for me in more than one way. I wasn't sure what was happening inside or outside of me, just that things were different.

I told Mom on the way home of the blood, and she told me that I had just become a woman. I didn't really understand what that meant. All I knew is that I'd spend the rest of that day watching the world fall apart on TV with a heating pad pressed up against my abdomen. By evening, I'd be screeching in pain, writhing around in bed as if taken over by a demon. I wondered, *This is what it feels like to be a woman?*

I didn't know then either that I'd spend the next few decades with cramps so debilitating each month that I'd vomit and faint and end up in a trance-like state from the pain before eventually collapsing in exhaustion. Painkillers offered only minimal relief.

I'd tell my gynecologists. They'd yawn and say, "Yeah, periods hurt."

"Yes, but . . ."

"Extra strength Tylenol and rest should help," they'd cut in. It seemed I had no other symptoms to warrant further testing.

I now know how severe the problem was because my labor contractions were significantly less painful than my monthly period cramps. I didn't know that what I was feeling was *labor* until an hour before my baby's head made its appearance outside my body.

Needless to say, my periods hurt. They felt burdensome when I had to take time off from work, the pain too excruciating to drive or attempt anything productive. Because of the shame attached to menstruation and consequently, lack of support for people with uteruses in society as a whole, I also felt the need to lie as to why I needed the day off for fear of being dismissed or disbelieved.

My periods also felt dirty. Like a secret I would be forced to hide for the rest of my life.

To make matters worse, the only theological connection I had for menstruation was that it was a *curse*. I was to suffer uncleanness and pain because Eve sinned in the garden of Eden. End of story. As women and as a society, we've played into this narrative, deriding ourselves and our bodies as a result. Bleeding is seen as a "condition" that needs to be hidden and endured instead of as an invitation to fullness and embodiment.

I heard once that painful menstruation can be understood as a result of the disconnection and dissociation we experience from our bodies and our reproductive organs. When we pick up the message that periods are negative, we see them as only a burden and a nuisance. Perhaps owning the energy flowing through our bodies during this time might give us the power to enjoy menstruation as a time of rejuvenation, newness, and rebirth—an opportunity to tap into a deeper part of ourselves that aligns with the moon and the tides.

Of course, it doesn't always feel this way, and disorders related to the menstrual cycle are to be taken seriously. But I often wonder if for decades my body was crying out, communicating something specific to me, inviting me to listen closely.

The word *menstruation* originates from the Greek word *mène* (moon) and the Latin *mensis* (month). A person's menstrual cycle mirrors the monthly lunar cycle.

Before menstrual journeys involved gynecologist offices, white coats, fluorescent lights, and stirrups, women had the moon and one another. They still bled and perhaps some writhed in pain, but they did so in the presence of feminine energy where women were attuned to each other's needs, fully in sync and solidarity. Instead of spending their monthly cycles alone in their homes, women lived in tribes where they would gather in menstrual tents each month and women of multiple generations cared for them. According to theologian Christy Bauman, Hebrew women dug holes in the ground, burying their first blood so that it could replenish the earth.[1] Throughout history, the bleeding of a woman has been understood as a holy and sacred experience.

Before our blood became our shame, "menstruation was held in high reverence."[2] Many Indigenous populations to this day believe that menstrual blood is a source of strength. In some Native American communities, men—because they don't have what they believe to be the portals of wisdom women have through monthly menstruation—actively seek out ways to experience this wisdom through sweat lodges and vision quests. Like childbirth, monthly menstruation was a way to tap into something divine and otherworldly. I once heard it told that in ancient Hawaiian communities, men could not get near women while they were bleeding because their intense spiritual power was too much for them to bear.

● ● ● ● ● ●

Luke 8 contains an incredible story of a bleeding woman who comes to Jesus because no doctor could help her. She touches his cloak and power is sucked right out of him—leaving his body and entering hers.

Right before this encounter, Jesus had healed the man possessed with an entire legion of demons simply by the power of his words. There was no touching. Only speaking. When news got out about what happened, the city and the countryside were in an uproar. Here was this man once a demoniac, now healed, once excluded from the community, now restored to belonging. But the people became afraid of Jesus because they did not understand. No longer bound with chains and restraints, this man was now whole. He was no longer their enemy, the one they could point to and whisper about. Perhaps it was the power Jesus contained in his body that frightened them. Not a power that destroys but a power that is stronger—and for some, more intimidating—a power that restores.

After this interaction, Jesus gets in a boat and heads back across the lake. Soon after arriving, crowds of people surround him and one among these is the bleeding woman, another body excluded from belonging. But this time, Jesus does not command; instead, it is the woman who pulls power from him. It is *her touch* that brings about her own healing.

In the ancient Greco-Roman world, there were gendered characteristics for healthy and sick bodies. I imagine these are the same sentiments that are carried forth today: men are strong and women are weak. Men's bodies (the ideal bodies) were thought of as healthy, and the characteristics associated with them were warmth and dryness. These bodies were seen as bound and impermeable. Women's bodies, on the other hand, were seen not only as weak but also as sickly. Our bodies were thought of as damp and porous. As a result, men were advised to stay away from the things that would expose them to these conditions— things like long baths, massages, and warm air. Excessive moisture on a man's skin was thought to make it soft, porous, and thus effeminate.[3]

Some theologians have pointed out that the flow of blood from the woman mirrors the flow of power from Jesus. Like the woman, unable to control the blood that leaks from her body, Jesus does not control the power that leaks from his. "Someone touched me," he said. "I know that power has gone out from me."

Both seemingly uncontrollable flows—the one of blood and the other of power—are "something embodied and physical," a thing that can be felt. Jesus and the woman feel the flows in their bodies begin and stop at the same moment.[4]

Naturally, she met all the categories of what it meant to be a woman: sickly, leaking, and even porous. But what does it mean that Jesus did too? He, like the brave, bleeding woman, leaked power the way she leaked blood.[5]

What can be said about a God who is not intimidated by possessing qualities that appear weak or effeminate? Perhaps in this way, Jesus cares to reverse the stigmas, the shame, perhaps even the toxic masculinity that might be attached to these things. After all, Jesus did not speak healing onto this woman the way he did with the man possessed by demons. Instead, the woman initiates her own healing, yanking it right out of him—a reversal of power dynamics as we understand them. She transgressed the rules to make an assertion of dignity, just like Jesus, who transgressed the rules to assert the dignity of those like her.[6]

And now the divine power that once belonged only to Jesus is hers: a power she took, a power he gladly gave away. Maybe it was there all along. Maybe it just needed to be reignited.

This bleeding woman is our patron saint of enacting our agency and taking back our power as bleeding women—a power already in us from the beginning, before our blood became a source of shame.

Women bleed as God bled. When we drink God's blood and eat God's flesh, we remember that our bodies are sacred, as God's body is sacred.

There is power in our blood too.

- What might the bleeding woman communicate to you about agency and the reversal of power dynamics?

A Birthing People

✱

Has the rain a father,
who brought forth drops of dew?
From whose womb does ice come;
who gave birth to heaven's frost?
—Job 38:28–29

In the beginning was a womb—dark, warm, and wet—and the Spirit hovered above it. The womb was without form until the Spirit breathed and it labored, and from the womb burst forth heaven and earth, land and sea, plant and animal, and last of all, humans. When it was done, God rested—cradling this creation. They whispered to each other: *In our image we created them.*

There's something carnal and wildly subversive about the fact that throughout the Bible, Father God is a birthing person. God is presented with a womb (e.g., Isa. 46:3); *he* gasps and pants on a birthing bed (Isa. 42:14); *he* labors to birth a child (Deut. 32:18).

This might make some folks uncomfortable, particularly those committed to prescribed "roles" for people, especially within the male-female binary. But as we've seen, God cannot be confined to those boxes. Likewise, the process of birthing is not tied exclusively to gender or sex organs. It is more expansive than that—a cosmic and universal reality. Birthing is not just something that happens in people with wombs. Birthing is also the process of creating. In this way, each of us in some capacity is involved in the work of birthing—of bringing to life something new—in ourselves and in each other.

This makes us not only birthing people but also midwives and doulas.

●･●･･●

Midwives and doulas are some of the oldest known vocations in history. In the ancient world, midwives were spiritual healers who not only delivered children but also prompted "magical" or religious protection over the mother and infant through rituals and spiritual practices.[1] Doulas were more informal, usually family or community members who helped support and guide those who were in labor. But as obstetric services became the norm, family and community members lost the necessary knowledge and confidence to assist in the birthing process.[2]

Together, midwives and doulas not only assist but also encourage, comfort, strengthen, remind, challenge, and advocate. This is true in birth, but isn't this also what we do for each other on the journey of what it means to be human?

I would not be where I am as a student, a daughter, a parent, a spouse, a friend, or a writer without the work of spiritual and emotional midwives and doulas in my life who have assisted me as I birthed ideas, degrees, books, projects, and humans. They've encouraged me when it felt as though I had reached a point where I could not go on. They've comforted me and lent their strength when weakness has set in. They've reminded me to breathe, to rest, to eat, to stay hydrated, to have fun. They've challenged me, supported me, and advocated for me.

My website belongs to me because a writer I nannied for in my early days of blogging encouraged me to purchase it for less than ten dollars. "You're going to need it when you publish your own book," she told me. "I know you will one day." I had never been published anywhere other than my Wordpress blog at this point, but I believe my success is due to her calling this out in me before I even knew it to be true in myself. This is what it means to act as a doula in someone's life, even if just in passing. This is what it means to belong to the human family. We need one another to survive and also to thrive—to journey into who we are supposed to become.

I purchased katarmas.com for a couple dollars that night while sitting at a writing desk not my own. My spiritual doula and I were both giddy with excitement.

Writer Alyssa Aldape talks about Christian calling this way: "I never had that mountaintop experience where I was told exactly what to do," she says. "But what I have had is people in my life who have tended to me and have seen my gifts and have been advocates for me in ways I couldn't see for myself yet."[3] Navigating this life requires that others hold our hands as we do the hard work of discovering and discerning and imagining who we could be.

What does it mean, then, that the Spirit of God is described as playing these exact same roles in our lives: supporter, encourager, and advocate? A God with a womb may not resonate with all of us as not all of us have birthed, but all of us were birthed once and all of us, in one way or another, are involved in a process of birthing. As image bearers of the divine, we are thus cocreators—midwives and doulas—for one another.

Birth itself is a process that serves "as the nucleus around which to build a paradigm for positive human interaction," writes professor and scholar Arisika Razak. The process of birthing—both physical and spiritual—reaches into the deepest parts of our being. Physical births carry significance for all people as human societies nurture and raise children. This also involves the process of bonding. She continues: "Spontaneous emotional bonding is a profound example of the human capacity for nurturing, love, and emotional attachment."[4] The process of birth is a process of human collaboration, co-creation, and connection.

We need midwives and doulas partly because the birthing process involves a whole lot of waiting. While it is exciting and anticipated, it happens slowly. Some people are in labor for twelve, twenty-four, even forty-eight hours before the moment finally arrives. While it may seem like nothing is happening on the outside, the baby is gradually making its way down the birth canal, somehow knowing how to be born. While those outside of the womb wait, the tiny life on the inside is preparing to emerge.

Isn't this also true of our becoming?

Our growth, our healing, even our creativity finds its way in and through us often gradually, incrementally. It can also appear to be hidden, stowed away somewhere inside of us and we're hoping like hell it'll emerge—soon. We may get impatient, but all along it is the doulas and midwives in our midst that discern that things are indeed moving, even when we cannot see or feel it. Sometimes we are too attached, to close to a thing, to see it objectively this way.

Almost inevitably there is a waiting process while what we are creating is gestating and taking shape. When the time is right, we are guided and tended as it births from inside us into the world, and if we're lucky, we get to do the guiding and tending for others who are crossing thresholds too. Birthing is a long practice that involves working with the whole person—mindbodyspirit. It involves being present throughout the entire process, offering support through every stage, even when it feels like "nothing is happening."

Like the divine, we are all birthing people, and we are all doulas and midwives, called to the sacred work of imagining, discerning, and naming things in others that they have yet to bring forth from themselves. Similarly, we remain expectant that in community, things will be called out in us that we wouldn't have named ourselves if we didn't have someone there to advocate, tend, or help us draw them out.

- Is something waiting to be birthed in you or in someone around you?
- Who has assisted you in the process of birthing, and what was this like? Similarly, how have you served in this role for others?

Day 40

The Sun Woman

✶

> But the earth helped the woman.
>
> —Revelation 12:16

What better way to end our forty-day journey than with the apocalypse?

In Greek, *apocalypse* literally means "an uncovering." And isn't this so fitting for what our situation often feels like? Wars, pandemics, and global political unrest only reveal and continue to expose the systems of domination and exploitation that have kept us all from our individual and collective flourishing. It is this very thing, I believe, that is at the heart of decolonization: an uncovering.

It's also the topic of the book of Revelation, which inspired the bestselling Left Behind series. Christians old and young have taken comfort in the idea of being "raptured" to heaven to escape the earth's grim fate. To be "left behind" on earth is every premillennial Christian kid's worst nightmare. But have you ever wondered what this message might have communicated about our world to a whole generation of people? Is the earth doomed—or worse yet, the devil's playground—as we have been told?

There are many commentaries that attempt to interpret the fantastic imagery found in John's apocalyptic vision, but there's one narrative in particular that catches my attention. Chapter 12 tells the story of "a woman clothed with the sun" (v. 1), the moon rests under her feet, a crown of twelve stars on her head. She is majestic, woven into the cosmos. She is also pregnant, vulnerable, and crying out from the pangs of labor. But to her horror and our surprise, she is not alone in her celestial dwelling.

Verse 3 introduces to the narrative a fiery red dragon with seven heads and ten horns, his power so great that his tail sweeps a third of the stars from the sky toward the earth. He too is an astonishing figure, one that is an enemy to the cosmos. The dragon is positioned in front of the woman. Like Mary, the mother of God, she is naked, bleeding, exposed. The voracious creature is ready to take advantage of her vulnerability. Worse, he is waiting for her child to emerge in order to devour it (v. 4). His seven heads each take a turn stalking, spewing misogyny, inciting evil.

The woman gives birth. But immediately her child is snatched up and taken to heaven. The Sun Woman then flees into the desert, "where God has prepared a place for her" (v. 6). Desert retreats were a common practice of Jewish sages and prophets. In our modern world, we often speak of the wilderness as a metaphor for hardship or distance from God—a place that represents darkness, loneliness, or desolation. But many characters in Scripture (from Abraham to Moses to Ezekiel to Hagar to Rizpah to Jesus and to Paul) were sent to the wilderness on purpose, not to suffer, but to be transformed by the natural world. The same is true for the Sun Woman. Under the traumatic circumstances, her wilderness sanctuary offers the perfect therapeutic environment: a place to grieve, to be nurtured, to heal.[1]

According to Greco-Roman sources, she's often referred to as the Queen of Heaven, surrounded by cosmic symbols in the manner of a goddess. The Greek goddess Artemis (known as Diana in the Roman pantheon) was depicted with the sun, moon, and stars as ornaments upon her—similar to the Sun Woman. A moon goddess, too, wore a crown of stars on her head.[2] Original audiences would have probably connected the celestial crown worn by the Sun Woman to the constellations of the ancient zodiac; recognizing her likeness to the Egyptian goddess Isis, "the beautiful essence of all the gods," who in the prior couple of centuries shaped the entire universe. Some liken the Sun Woman to the figure of Chokmah, or Wisdom, who "was formed . . . at the beginning, before the earth was (Prov. 8:23)."[3]

The story then turns to a cosmic battle in heaven between Michael the archangel and the dragon, who is thrown down to earth. To the original audience, the depiction of warfare in the cosmos spoke to the struggles they faced in regard to the powers of empire, which raped and ravaged not just their people but the whole earth—her land and her resources.[4] Apocalyptic literature doesn't simply look toward a new world; instead, it laments the destructiveness of our own.[5]

Just as John witnessed the havoc that empire was wreaking on land and on peoples when he penned this vision, we too experience the effects of empire causing chaos in our age. Mining, deforestation, and the like are polluting and devastating, littering and poisoning. "We see climate change melting ice and glaciers, fertile lands turning into deserts, toxic runoffs destroying the habitats of millions of marine creatures, and wild weather events ruining human communities."[6] Like the dragon ravaging the cosmos, empire and the effects of capitalism are devastating our own world.

But the story doesn't end there. When the dragon sees that the Queen of Heaven has retreated to earth, he proceeds to chase her, persistent in his thirst for blood. Like empire, he is unrelenting in his pursuit of violence. While being chased, however, the woman is given wings "of the great eagle" so she can fly to her place in the desert (Rev. 12:14). Eagles' wings are an ancient prototype of liberation; they represent flights from oppression. "I bore you on eagle's wings," says God to the people after they escape yet another "infant-murdering grip"[7] under the pharaoh of Egypt (Exod. 19:4).

As the woman flies away, the dragon makes a final attempt to destroy her by pouring a river after her so that it might sweep her away in the same way as Pharaoh's army was swept away by the Red Sea. But something incredible happens, often overlooked in traditional readings of Revelation. The text literally reads, "The earth helped the woman" (12:16).

The earth—in all her wisdom—opens her mouth, swallowing the river. She shuts the dragon's mouth once and for all, preventing it from spewing out more evil.

But this isn't the only time the earth uses her wisdom for justice. Theologian Brigitte Kahl notes that in Genesis, the earth opens her mouth for the first time to take in the blood of Abel so that it may "cry out" in protest (4:10) against Cain. The earth, herself, takes the side of the weak and victimized, calling out Cain's murderous act, deception, and denial.[8]

No longer passive, the earth becomes a proxy of liberation for the suffering woman and an active agent of opposition against the "logic and law of empire with all its ecocidal, fratricidal and suicidal implications."[9] The earth participates in caretaking and resistance, but unlike empire, her resistance is nonviolent. Both the earth and the woman are "givers of life perceived as a threat to the dominant powers." They are welded together in a bond of solidarity. Earth is the reason for the Sun Woman's survival, saving her from death for peace and respite in the wilderness where she will be nurtured and cared for.[10]

The bond of solidarity between the woman and the earth only infuriates the dragon more, so he goes off to make war with the rest of her children. This woman is not just any woman; she is personified as our mother. In this apocalyptic and cosmic vision, the earth and our mythical mother with a crown of stars work together to birth and resist, to nurture and take care.

John's revelation aims at the possibility of a different world—one disentangled from the evils of empire that stalk and kill—where our Sun Mother and her children, our siblings, are in close connection to our Earth Mother.

● ·· ● ·· ●

Our journey began in the fertile land in Genesis and ends with fertile land in the Revelation vision. The tree of life stands in the middle of the Great City, its leaves and ceaseless harvest of fruit heal and nourish the nations. It is an image of "sustainable integration of urbanity and ecology."[11] There's a river here, but this time it is of life, pouring from the throne of God.

This image of wholeness, sustainability, and fertility is what leads us to nurture and care for our world through the divine feminine in us; like mothers, midwives, and doulas—spiritual and physical—we birth forth new life with our hands and with our hearts. May we truly live an "on earth as it is in heaven" reality, a cosmic vision of anti-imperialistic creaturely flourishing.

This is sacred belonging.

CONCLUSION

The writing of this manuscript saw many seasons. I began writing ferociously during the winter months. My fingers—bare, cold, and frail—banged against the keyboard, resembling the bare branches that decorated the sky like veins. These days were slow, short, and sleepy, but magical nonetheless. Just when I began to tire from bundling up, longing for warmth, the clouds sprinkled me with their fairy dust. It was hard to write on those days, with my attention glued to the sea of white outside my window. I gave myself grace on snow days, pouring myself an extra cup of coffee, lingering in my PJs a little longer.

I trucked away through spring when the weather was just right. The starling and the sparrow were busy too, as they began building their nests from the gifts of the earth, singing their truths to one another while they did it. I took writing breaks at the park down the way, where baby swans decorated the lake like stars. Each one a promise, a twinkle of hope. These days were longer, busier.

As summer got closer, the days became wetter and longer still. Sometimes we waited anxiously inside. It was bittersweet, knowing we had to pause what we were doing so the earth could replenish. We watched the leaves bounce and dance under the droplets of water. Sometimes we joined them. The birds bathed. The world slowed, I loved writing on those days.

And then the heat began settling in, weighing heavy on us. We spent these days eating ice cream at the public pool. My skin glistened. I smelled of chlorine. I was happy. I found myself wringing words from my body like water from a wet beach towel. Inspiration found me on those summer days.

It is now autumn. The leaves are making their way to the earth, where they will spend the rest of their days becoming one with the soil.

I've sat at this same desk for most of this time, watching my neighbors shift, too, with each season. I step outside regularly to chat with them. Very often our conversation is about the weather.

I've learned to love talking about the weather. But I admit, I wasn't always a fan of it. Like many of us, I'd roll my eyes at the thought of chatting up a stranger about the temperature outside or the impending rain. I'd dismiss it as small talk, unimportant—a shallow kind of conversation. It was awkwardness, I thought. Trivial. Aren't there more important things to talk about?

It may seem this way to those of us privileged to be able to eat strawberries year-round. We've become so disconnected from the process it takes to get food on our plates that we forget that to the majority of the world—to our ancestors—the rain or lack thereof, the slight shift in season, the lightning and the thunder, are everything. They represent life and death, deprivation and sustenance.

To notice the weather is to speak to an embodied way of being; it is to recognize our connection to all created things. This is exactly how I wanted to end this devotional: talking about the weather and how it affected me and my writing. Perhaps reclaiming this "small talk" can be part of our decolonizing journey and a way to connect more deeply to our ancestors.

What if we made it a practice to talk about the weather deliberately and with intention? What if we remembered our place, our privilege, our connection to the natural world when we greet each other with "It's a beautiful day, isn't it?"

Doing so might encourage us to notice, to pay attention, to honor those of us who have long been at the mercy of Mother Nature.

Doing so might remind us that we belong to one another.

NOTES

Introduction

1. Kwok Pui-lan, *Postcolonial Imagination and Feminist Theology* (Louisville: Westminster John Knox, 2005), 2.

2. Richard Horsley, "Submerged Biblical Histories and Imperial Biblical Studies," in *The Postcolonial Bible*, ed. R. S. Sugirtharajah (Sheffield, UK: Sheffield Academic, 1998), 154–55.

3. Carol J. Adams, ed., *Ecofeminism and the Sacred* (New York: Continuum, 1993), 4.

4. For passages on other gods, see 1 Kings 11:33; Exod. 12:12, 15:11; Pss. 82:1, 95:3.

Day 1 Sacred Belonging

1. Evan, "The Threat of Reintroduced Wolves to Livestock in Yellowstone," Debating Science Course Blog, University of Massachusetts Amherst, December 2, 2015, https://blogs.umass.edu/natsci397a-eross/the-threat-of-reintroduced-wolves-to-livestock-in-yellowstone/.

2. Peter Wohlleben, *The Secret Wisdom of Nature: Trees, Animals, and the Extraordinary Balance of All Living Things*, trans. Jane Billinghurst (Vancouver: Greystone Books, 2019), 6–10.

Day 2 The Creatures Teach Us

1. Tom Huizenga, "How Do You Bond with Mozart? Adopt a Starling," NPR, April 20, 2017, https://www.npr.org/sections/deceptivecadence/2017/04/20/524349771/how-do-you-bond-with-mozart-adopt-a-starling.

2. Barbara Brown Taylor, *The Preaching Life* (Cambridge, MA: Cowley Publications, 1993), 47.

3. Richard Rohr, *The Universal Christ: How a Forgotten Reality Can Change Everything We See, Hope for, and Believe* (New York: Convergent Books, 2019), 58.

4. Patty Krawec, *Becoming Kin: An Indigenous Call to Unforgetting the Past and Reimaging Our Future* (Minneapolis: Broadleaf Books, 2022), 27.

Day 3 The Mountains Groan

1. Jeremy Punt, *Postcolonial Biblical Interpretation: Reframing Paul*, Studies in Theology and Religion (Boston: Brill, 2015), 203.

2. Punt, *Postcolonial Biblical Interpretation*, 204.

3. Sandra L. Richter, *Stewards of Eden: What Scripture Says about the Environment and Why It Matters* (Downers Grove, IL: InterVarsity, 2020), 22.

4. Joanna Macy, "Climate Crisis as a Spiritual Path," YouTube documentary, accessed December 31, 2022, https://www.youtube.com/watch?v=bQAYVKqTkKo.

5. Macy, "Climate Crisis as a Spiritual Path."

Day 4 A Wild World beyond Us

1. Peter Wohlleben, *The Secret Wisdom of Nature: Trees, Animals, and the Extraordinary Balance of All Living Things*, trans. Jane Billinghurst (Vancouver: Greystone Books, 2019), loc. 120, Kindle

2. Wohlleben, *Secret Wisdom of Nature*, loc. 81, Kindle.

3. Randy Woodley, *Shalom and the Community of Creation: An Indigenous Vision* (Grand Rapids: Eerdmans, 2012), 54.

Day 5 Our Soulful Companions

1. See, e.g., Gen. 1:20–21, 24, 30; 2:19; 9:10, 12, 15–16; Lev. 11:46.

2. Richard Rohr, *The Universal Christ: How a Forgotten Reality Can Change Everything We See, Hope for, and Believe* (New York: Convergent Books, 2019), vii.

Day 6 Creation Rejoices

1. Robin Wall Kimmerer, *Braiding Sweetgrass: Indigenous Wisdom, Scientific Knowledge, and the Teachings of Plants* (Minneapolis: Milkweed, 2013), 295.

2. Wendell Berry and Ellen Davis, "The Art of Being Creatures," *On Being* podcast with Krista Tippett, June 10, 2010, https://onbeing.org/programs/wendell-berry-ellen-davis-the-art-of-being-creatures/.

3. Ellen F. Davis, *Getting Involved with God: Rediscovering the Old Testament* (Lanham, MD: Rowman & Littlefield, 2001), 126.

4. James H. Cone, "Whose Earth Is It Anyway?" *CrossCurrents* 50, no. 1/2 (2000): 41–42, available at http://www.jstor.org/stable/24461228.

5. Kimmerer, *Braiding Sweetgrass*, 327.

Day 7 A Kin-dom of Reciprocity

1. See Amy-Jill Levine, *Short Stories by Jesus: The Enigmatic Parables of a Controversial Rabbi* (Nashville: Abingdon, 2018).

2. Levine, *Short Stories by Jesus*, 7.

3. Wendell Berry and Ellen Davis, "The Art of Being Creatures," *On Being* podcast with Krista Tippett, June 10, 2010, https://onbeing.org/programs/wendell-berry-ellen-davis-the-art-of-being-creatures/.

4. Robin Wall Kimmerer, *Braiding Sweetgrass: Indigenous Wisdom, Scientific Knowledge, and the Teachings of Plants* (Minneapolis: Milkweed, 2013), 115.

Day 8 Earth, Wind, Fire, Water

1. Nicodemus's encounter with Jesus is relayed in John 3:1–21.

2. Jesus's conversation with the woman by the well can be found in John 4:4–27.

3. Christine Valters Paintner, *Water, Wind, Earth, and Fire: The Christian Practice of Praying with the Elements* (Notre Dame, IN: Sorin Books, 2010), 4.

4. Thomas Merton, *The Intimate Merton*, ed. Patrick Hart and Jonathan Montaldo (New York: HarperCollins, 1999), 80.

5. Paintner, *Water, Wind, Earth, and Fire*, 114.

6. Paintner, *Water, Wind, Earth, and Fire*, 138.

Day 9 Ghost Stories

1. Sze-kar Wan, "Where Have All the Ghosts Gone? Evolution of a Concept in Biblical Literature," in *Rethinking Ghosts in World Religions*, ed. Mu-Chou Poo, Numen Books Series (Leiden: Brill, 2009), 62.

2. Rabbi Mike Uram, "Jewish Ghost Stories and the Walking Dead," *Philadelphia Inquirer*, October 29, 2014, https://www.inquirer.com/philly/columnists/mike_uram /Rabbi_Uram_Jewish_ghost_stories.html.

3. See Steven Shankman, "Ghosts and Responsibility: The Hebrew Bible, Confucius, Plato," in Poo, *Rethinking Ghosts in World Religions*, 82–83.

4. This isn't the only place in the Bible where the disciples encounter Jesus and believe him to be a ghost (see Luke 24:37).

5. Flannery O'Connor, *Letters of a Nation: A Collection of Extraordinary American Letters*, ed. Andrew Carroll (New York: Broadway Books, 1997), 411.

Day 10 What Do You Want?

1. Howard Thurman, "The Sound of the Genuine," baccalaureate address at Spelman College, May 4, 1980, *The Spelman Messenger* 96, no. 4 (Summer 1980), 14–15, https://www.uindy.edu/eip/files/reflection4.pdf.

2. Thurman, "Sound of the Genuine."

3. Lisa Colón DeLay, *The Wild Land Within: Cultivating Wholeness through Spiritual Practice* (Minneapolis: Broadleaf Books, 2021), 2.

4. Henri Nouwen, *Reaching Out: The Three Movements of the Spiritual Life* (New York: Doubleday, 1975), 40.

Day 11 Native Conversations

1. See Kat Armas, "The Bible and the Verb of God," Made for Pax, StoryArc 3, accessed December 31, 2022, https://www.madeforpax.org/scripture/myth#kat-armas.

2. See Victoria Loorz, *Church of the Wild: How Nature Invites Us into the Sacred* (Minneapolis: Broadleaf Books, 2021), 106–7.

3. See Brené Brown, *Atlas of the Heart: Mapping Meaningful Connection and the Language of Human Experience* (New York: Random House, 2021), xxi.

4. See Armas, "The Bible and the Verb of God."

5. Willie James Jennings, *Acts: A Theological Commentary on the Bible*, Belief Commentaries on the Bible (Louisville: Westminster John Knox, 2017), 1.

6. Jennings, *Acts*, 28.

Day 12 Lingering in the Tension

1. Emily Freeman (@emilypfreeman), "It's the season of the in-between," *Instagram*, March 5, 2022, https://www.instagram.com/p/CauSXlMup86/.

2. Katherine May, *Wintering: The Power of Rest and Retreat in Difficult Times* (New York: Riverhead Books, 2020), 168.

3. May, *Wintering*, 169.

Day 13 Arguing with God

1. Jonathan Sacks, *Rabbi Jonathan Sacks's Haggadah: Hebrew and English Text with New Essays and Commentary* (Jerusalem: Maggid Books, 2015), 106.

2. Anson Laytner, *Arguing with God: A Jewish Tradition* (Northvale, NJ: J. Aronson, 1990), 38.

3. Laytner, *Arguing with God*, 38.

4. Sacks, *Rabbi Jonathan Sacks's Haggadah*, 107.

5. Brené Brown, *Atlas of the Heart: Mapping Meaningful Connection and the Language of Human Experience* (New York: Random House, 2021), xviii.

Day 14 The Gift of Dreams

1. Deirdre Barrett, "The Science of Dreaming," *Speaking of Psychology* podcast, American Psychological Association, December 2018, https://www.apa.org/news/podcasts/speaking-of-psychology/science-of-dreaming.

2. As told in Bonnelle Lewis Strickling, *Dreaming about the Divine* (Albany: State University of New York Press, 2007), 5.

3. Alessandro Casale, "Indigenous Dreams: Prophetic Nature, Spirituality, and Survivance," Indigenous New Hampshire Collaborative Collective, January 25, 2019, https://indigenousnh.com/2019/01/25/indigenous-dreams/.

4. Kate Kellaway, "When We Dream, We Have the Perfect Chemical Canvas for Intense Visions," *The Guardian*, April 14, 2019, https://www.theguardian.com/science/2019/apr/14/dreams-perfect-canvas-intense-visions-alice-robb-interview.

5. Alice Robb, *Why We Dream: The Transformative Power of Our Nightly Journey* (New York: Mariner Books, 2019), 8.

6. Jill Hammer, *Grounding in Our Dreams: How Dreams Connect Us to the Cosmos and Ourselves*, Ayin Press, accessed December 32, 2022, https://ayinpress.org/grounding-in-our-dreams/.

7. Hammer, *Grounding in Our Dreams*.

8. Robb, *Why We Dream*, 8.

Day 16 A Deeper Dimension

1. Flannery O'Connor, *Mystery and Manners* (New York: Farrar, Straus & Giroux, 1969), 124.

2. Krista Tippett, *Becoming Wise: An Inquiry into the Mystery and Art of Living* (New York: Penguin Books, 2017), 162.

3. Steven Charleston, *The Four Vision Quests of Jesus* (New York: Morehouse, 2015), 36.

Day 17 A Disabled God

1. Hillary L. McBride, *The Wisdom of Your Body: Finding Healing, Wholeness, and Connection through Embodied Living* (Grand Rapids: Brazos, 2021), 14–16.

2. Nancy Eisland, *The Disabled God: Toward a Liberatory Theology of Disability* (Nashville: Abingdon, 1994), 100.

3. Rabbi Julia Watts Belser, "God on Wheels: Disability Leadership and Spiritual Leadership," YouTube, October 24, 2019, Yale Divinity School, https://www.youtube.com/watch?app=desktop&v=tjq7sWgwsQk.

Day 18 Getting Curious

1. Arthur Haines, *A New Path: To Transcend the Great Forgetting through Incorporating Ancestral Practices into Contemporary Living* (Canton, ME: V. F. Thomas Co., 2017), 166.

2. Haines, *A New Path*, 167.

3. Haines, *A New Path*, 167.

4. Celeste Ng, quoted in Carolina De Robertis, ed., *Radical Hope: Letters of Love and Dissent in Dangerous Times* (New York: Vintage Books, 2017), 223.

5. Mary Oliver, "The Summer Day," in *New and Selected Poems: Volume One* (Boston: Beacon, 1990), 94.

Day 19 Breath Prayer

1. Nancy S. Wiens, "Breath Prayer: An Ancient Spiritual Practice Connected with Science," BioLogos, July 1, 2019, https://biologos.org/articles/breath-prayer-an-ancient-spiritual-practice-connected-with-science.

Day 20 God Moves In

1. Shannan Martin, *Start with Hello: And Other Simple Ways to Live as Neighbors* (Grand Rapids: Revell, 2022), 43, 14.

2. Mihee Kim-Kort, "Reflections on the Lectionary," *Christian Century* 139, no. 5 (2022): 20.

Day 21 Reawakening Your Wildness

1. Howard Zinn, *A People's History of the United States: 1492–Present* (New York: HarperPerennial, 2015), 4.

2. Kat Armas, *Abuelita Faith: What Women on the Margins Teach Us about Wisdom, Persistence, and Strength* (Grand Rapids: Brazos, 2021), 154.

3. For more on body-shame, body-oppression, and radical self-love, see Sonya Renee Taylor, *The Body Is Not an Apology: The Power of Radical Self-Love,* 2nd ed. (Oakland, CA: Berrett-Koehler, 2021).

4. Brené Brown, "Shame vs. Guilt," January 15, 2013, https://brenebrown.com /articles/2013/01/15/shame-v-guilt/.

5. Daniel J. Donohue, "Sacred Nakedness Narraphor: The Untold Story of Shame and Glory," (PhD diss., George Fox University, 2015), 79, https://digitalcommons .georgefox.edu/cgi/viewcontent.cgi article=1095&context=dmin.

Day 22 Eyes of Abundance

1. Lois Tverberg, "A Good Eye or a Bad Eye? A Cryptic but Critical Idiom," Our Rabbi Jesus, January 2, 2019, https://ourrabbijesus.com/articles/a-good-eye-or-a-bad -eye-a-cryptic-but-critical-idiom/.

2. Lois Tverberg, *Walking in the Dust of Rabbi Jesus: How the Jewish Words of Jesus Can Change Your Life* (Grand Rapids: Zondervan, 2012), 69–79.

3. For more on a scarcity mindset, see the toolkit created by Emily Chen, Jenny Dorsey, Sarah Hong, and Sarah Koff, "Scarcity Mentality Affects Marginalized Groups Differently—So How Does It Manifest for Asian Americans," Studio ATAO, May 5, 2022, https://www.studioatao.org/scarcity.

Day 23 A Question of Embodiment

1. Marty Solomon, "Jonah—Potential," *BEMA Discipleship* podcast 52, November 16, 2017, https://www.bemadiscipleship.com/52.

2. Solomon, "Jonah—Potential."

3. Solomon, "Jonah—Potential."

4. Ruby Sales, "Where Does It Hurt?," *On Being* podcast with Krista Tippett, September 15, 2016, https://onbeing.org/programs/ruby-sales-where-does-it-hurt/.

5. Hillary L. McBride, *The Wisdom of Your Body: Finding Healing, Wholeness, and Connection through Embodied Living* (Grand Rapids: Brazos, 2021), 38–39.

Day 24 God amid the Crowds

1. Wille James Jennings, *After Whiteness: An Education in Belonging* (Grand Rapids: Eerdmans, 2020), 24.

2. Jennings, *After Whiteness,* 13.

Day 25 The *Genius Loci*

1. Lara Medina, "Creating Sacred Space," in *Voices from the Ancestors: Xicanx and Latinx Spiritual Expressions and Healing Practices,* ed. Lara Medina and Martha R. Gonzales (Tucson: University of Arizona Press, 2019), 37.

2. David Whyte, *Consolations: The Solace, Meaning, and Nourishment of Everyday Words*, rev. ed. (Langley, WA: Many Rivers Press, 2021), 51.

3. Whyte, *Consolations*, 51.

4. Whyte, *Consolations*, 51.

Day 26 Eternal Life

1. Rabbi Danielle Upbin, "Beginning the Amidah by Connecting to Our Ancestors," My Jewish Learning, accessed December 31, 2022, https://www.myjewishlearning.com/article/beginning-the-amidah-by-connecting-to-our-ancestors/.

2. Rachel Held Evans with Jeff Chu, *Wholehearted Faith* (New York: Harper One, 2021), 22.

3. Yreina D. Cervántez, "Lamento Cihuateteo: Llanto de Juárez," in *Voices from the Ancestors: Xicanx and Latinx Spiritual Expressions and Healing Practices*, ed. Lara Medina and Martha R. Gonzales (Tucson: University of Arizona Press, 2019), 153.

4. Aaron Freeman, "Planning Ahead Can Make a Difference in the End," NPR, June 1, 2005, https://www.npr.org/templates/story/story.php?storyId=4675953.

5. Karen González, "Ancestral Wisdom: Communing with Our Ancestors," *Café with Comadres* podcast 7, October 2021, https://open.spotify.com/episode/6PI69i6Ni5XIE3GdquUfjk.

Day 27 Our Celestial Siblings

1. Kocku von Stuckrad, "Jewish and Christian Astrology in Late Antiquity: A New Approach," *Numen* 47, no. 1 (2000): 6.

2. James H. Charlesworth, "Jewish Astrology in the Talmud, Pseudepigrapha, the Dead Sea Scrolls, and Early Palestinian Synagogues," *Harvard Theological Review* 70, no. 3/4 (1977): 193.

3. See, e.g., Gen. 15:5, 22:17, and 26:4.

4. Walter C. Kaiser Jr., Peter H. Davids, F. F. Bruce, and Manfred Brauch, *Hard Sayings of the Bible* (Downers Grove, IL: InterVarsity Press, 2010).

5. Chet Raymo, "Do You See What I See?," Science Musings, February 24, 2022, https://www.sciencemusings.com/do-you-see-what-i-see/.

6. Raymo, "Do You See What I See?"

Day 28 The Cycle of Time

1. Robin Wall Kimmerer, *Braiding Sweetgrass: Indigenous Wisdom, Scientific Knowledge, and the Teachings of Plants* (Minneapolis: Milkweed, 2013), 232.

2. Marty Solomon, "Trust the Story," *Bema Discipleship* podcast 1, September 8, 2016, https://www.bemadiscipleship.com/1.

Day 29 Rooted in Place

1. Monica Jyotsna Melanchthon, "Seeking the Peace and Prosperity of the City: The Politics of Jeremiah 29:1, 4–7," Political Theology Network, October 7, 2013, https://

politicaltheology.com/seeking-the-peace-and-prosperity-of-the-city-the-politics-of
-jeremiah-2914-7/.

2. Maria Popova, "How Naming Confers Dignity upon Life and Gives Meaning
to Existence," *The Marginalian*, July 23, 2105, https://www.themarginalian.org/2015
/07/23/robin-wall-kimmerer-gathering-moss-naming/.

3. Popova, "How Naming Confers Dignity."

4. Popova, "How Naming Confers Dignity."

5. Robin Wall Kimmerer, *Braiding Sweetgrass: Indigenous Wisdom, Scientific Knowledge, and the Teachings of Plants* (Minneapolis: Milkweed, 2013), 207.

Day 30 A New Moon

1. Sarah Faith Gottesdiener, *The Moon Book: Lunar Magic to Change Your Life* (New
York: St. Martin's Press, 2020), 3.

Day 31 The Prophets in Our Midst

1. Shannon K. Evans, *Rewilding Motherhood: Your Path to an Empowered Feminine
Spirituality* (Grand Rapids: Brazos, 2021), 62.

Day 32 The Cardinal Directions

1. "Medicine Ways: Traditional Healers and Healing," Native Voices, accessed December 31, 2022, https://www.nlm.nih.gov/nativevoices/exhibition/healing-ways
/medicine-ways/medicine-wheel.html.

2. Lara Medina, "Honoring the Sacred Directions," in *Voices from the Ancestors:
Xicanx and Latinx Spiritual Expressions and Healing Practices*, ed. Lara Medina and
Martha R. Gonzales (Tucson: University of Arizona Press, 2019), 31–32.

3. Ángel Manuel Rodríguez, "The Symbolism of the Four Cardinal Directions,"
Seventh-day Adventist Church, accessed December 31, 2022, https://www.adven
tistbiblicalresearch.org/materials/the-symbolism-of-the-four-cardinal-directions/.

4. Christine Valters Paintner, *Water, Wind, Earth, and Fire: The Christian Practice of
Praying with the Elements* (Notre Dame, IN: Sorin Books, 2010), 6.

5. Robin Wall Kimmerer, *Braiding Sweetgrass: Indigenous Wisdom, Scientific Knowledge, and the Teachings of Plants* (Minneapolis: Milkweed, 2013), 208.

6. Kimmerer, *Braiding Sweetgrass*, 209.

7. Reuven Chaim Klein, "Looking Four Directions," Ohr Somayach, December 3,
2016, https://ohr.edu/this_week/talmud_tips/7117.

8. "The Four Directions and Medicine Wheel of Native Americans," Gaia, September 17, 2020, https://www.gaia.com/article/four-directions.

9. Rodríguez, "Symbolism of the Four Cardinal Directions."

10. "Four Directions and Medicine Wheel of Native Americans."

11. Medina, "Honoring the Sacred Directions," 32.

12. Medina, "Honoring the Sacred Directions," 32.

Day 33 Pachamama

1. Merlin Stone, *When God Was a Woman* (New York: Dial Press, 1976), xiii.

2. Rosemary Radford Ruether, *Women Healing Earth: Third World Women on Ecology, Feminism, and Religion*, Ecology and Justice (Maryknoll, NY: Orbis Books, 1996), 4.

3. Anibal Quijano, "Coloniality of Power, Eurocentrism, and Latin America," *Nepantla: Views from the South* 1, no. 3 (2000): 216.

4. Carol J. Adams, ed., *Ecofeminism and the Sacred* (New York: Continuum, 1993), 1.

5. Ruether, *Women Healing Earth*, 6.

6. Emilie Townes, "To Be Called Beloved: Womanist Ontology in PostModern Refraction," *The Annual of the Society of Christian Ethics* 13 (1993): 101.

7. Elaine Wainwright, *Women Healing/Healing Women: The Genderisation of Healing in Early Christianity*, Bible World (New York: Routledge, 2014), 134.

8. Wainwright, *Women Healing/Healing Women*, 157.

9. Wainwright, *Women Healing/Healing Women*, 134.

10. Ruether, *Women Healing Earth*, 4.

Day 34 The Real Thing

1. Sarah Bessey, *Jesus Feminist: An Invitation to Revisit the Bible's View of Women* (New York: Howard Books, 2013), loc. 115, Kindle.

2. KJ Ramsey (@kjramseywrites), "The Word became flesh through the womb of a woman," Instagram, August 15, 2022, https://www.instagram.com/p/ChTKu WbpAPh/.

Day 35 The Power of the Erotic

1. Abi Doukhan, *Womanist Wisdom in the Song of Songs: Secrets of an African Princess* (Cham, Switzerland: Palgrave MacMillan, 2019), 4–5.

2. Carol Meyers, "Gender Imagery in the Song of Songs" in *A Feminist Companion to the Song of Songs*, ed. Athalya Brenner (1993; repr., Sheffield: Sheffield Academic Press, 2001), 204.

3. Doukhan, *Womanist Wisdom in the Song of Songs*, 19.

4. Doukhan, *Womanist Wisdom in the Song of Songs*, 19.

5. Audre Lorde, "Uses of the Erotic," in *Sister Outsider: Essays and Speeches*, rev. ed., Crossing Press Feminist Series (Berkeley: Crossing Press, 2007), 41.

6. Wille James Jennings, *After Whiteness: An Education in Belonging* (Grand Rapids: Eerdmans, 2020), 11.

7. Rita Nakashima Brock, *Journeys by Heart: A Christology of Erotic Power* (New York: Crossroad, 1988), 26.

8. Lorde, "Uses of the Erotic," 44.

Day 36 The Breasted One

1. Florence Williams, *Breasts: A Natural and Unnatural History* (New York: Norton, 2013), 2.

2. Williams, *Breasts*, 12.

3. Shannon K. Evans, *Rewilding Motherhood: Your Path to an Empowered Feminine Spirituality* (Grand Rapids: Brazos, 2021), 103.

4. Augustine, *Homilies on 1 John* 3.1, in *A Select Library of Nicene and Post-Nicene Fathers of the Christian Church*, 1st series, ed. Philip Schaff (repr., Peabody, MA: Hendrickson, 2004), 7:476.

5. John Chrysostom, "Homilies on the Gospel of St. Matthew," quoted in Cassian Folsom, "The Effects of the Eucharist in the Writings of Four Fathers," *Antiphon: A Journal for Liturgical Renewal* 24, no. 3 (2020): 298.

6. David Biale, "The God with Breasts: El Shaddai in the Bible" *History of Religions* 21, no. 3 (1982): 247.

7. Julian of Norwich, *Revelations of Divine Love*, ed. Barry Windeatt (Oxford: Oxford University Press, 2015), 130.

Day 37 Primary Issues

1. Phyllis Trible calls these neglected stories "texts of terror." See Trible's *Texts of Terror: Literary-Feminist Readings of the Biblical Narratives*, 40th anniversary ed. (Minneapolis: Fortress, 2022).

Day 38 Uncontrollable Flows

1. Christy Angelle Bauman, *Theology of the Womb: Knowing God through the Body of a Woman* (Eugene, OR: Cascade Books, 2019), 20.

2. Shannon K. Evans, *Rewilding Motherhood: Your Path to an Empowered Feminine Spirituality* (Grand Rapids: Brazos, 2021), 101.

3. Candida R. Moss, "The Man with the Flow of Power: Porous Bodies in Mark 5:25–34," *Journal of Biblical Literature* 129, no. 3 (Fall 2010): 513.

4. Moss, "Man with the Flow of Power," 516.

5. Moss, "Man with the Flow of Power," 508.

6. Alease A. Brown, "Bleeding Women and Theology from Below," *Stellenbosch Theological Journal* 6, no. 4 (2020): 13–36.

Day 39 A Birthing People

1. Kat Armas, *Abuelita Faith: What Women on the Margins Teach Us about Wisdom, Persistence, and Strength* (Grand Rapids: Brazos, 2021), 60.

2. Coburn Dukehart, "Doulas, Exploring a Tradition of Support," NPR, July 14, 2011, https://www.npr.org/sections/babyproject/2011/07/14/137827923/doulas -exploring-a-tradition-of-support.

3. Alyssa Aldape, "On Power, Calling, and *Encanto*," *Protagonistas* podcast with Kat Armas, February 24, 2022, https://katarmas.com/theprotagonistaspodcast.

4. Arisika Razak, "Healing Ourselves, Healing the Planet," in *Reweaving the World: The Emergence of Ecofeminism*, ed. Irene Diamond and Gloria Feman Orenstein (San Francisco: Sierra Club Books, 1990), 166.

Day 40 The Sun Woman

1. Catherine Keller, *Facing Apocalypse: Climate, Democracy and Other Last Chances* (Maryknoll, NY: Orbis Books, 2021), 43.

2. Craig R. Koester, *Revelation: A New Translation with Introduction and Commentary*, Anchor Bible (New Haven: Yale University Press, 2014), 528.

3. Keller, *Facing Apocalypse*, 43.

4. Elaine Wainwright, "Read the Signs of the Times: Revelation 11:19; 12:1–6, 10–12," *Tui Motu* magazine, July 31, 2018, https://hail.to/tui-motu-interislands-mag azine/article/tIsdGRD.

5. Keller, *Facing Apocalypse*, 43.

6. Wainwright, "Read the Signs of the Times."

7. Brigitte Kahl, "Gaia, Polis, and *Ekklēsia* at the Miletus Market Gate: An Ecocritical Reimagination of Revelation 12:16," in *The First Urban Churches 1: Methodological Foundations*, ed. James R. Harrison and L. L. Welborn, Writings from the Greco-Roman World Supplement (Atlanta: SBL Press, 2015), 119.

8. Kahl, "Gaia, Polis, and *Ekklēsia*, 145.

9. Kahl, "Gaia, Polis, and *Ekklēsia*, 144.

10. Kahl, "Gaia, Polis, and *Ekklēsia*, 115–17.

11. Kahl, "Gaia, Polis, and *Ekklēsia*, 145.

Kat Armas (MDiv and MAT, Fuller Theological Seminary), a Cuban-American writer and speaker, hosts the *Protagonistas* podcast, where she highlights stories of everyday women of color, including writers, pastors, church leaders, and theologians. She is the author of *Abuelita Faith* and has written for *Plough* magazine, *The Christian Century, Christianity Today, Sojourners, Relevant,* Christians for Biblical Equality, Fuller Youth Institute, *Fathom* magazine, and Missio Alliance. Armas speaks regularly at conferences on race and justice and lives in Nashville.